IRELAND'S
WILD COUNTRYSIDE

Over much of the west of Ireland a thin blanket of peat covers the entire landscape stretching from the summits of the hills right down to sea level. In all of Europe this habitat type is found only in Ireland and Scotland, on the rain-washed fringes of the Atlantic Ocean.

IRELAND'S
WILD COUNTRYSIDE

ÉAMON de BUITLÉAR

TIGER BOOKS INTERNATIONAL
LONDON

Do Lailí

_____

Acknowledgments

*My very special thanks to Richard Nairn, who persuaded me
to undertake this project and acted with considerable enthusiasm and dedication
in his role as scientific adviser for the entire book.
I would also like to thank the following individuals for their much valued help
and guidance with parts of the book. Dr Rory Harrington, Jim Ryan and
Caitríona Douglas (National Parks and Wildlife Service, Office of Public Works),
Dr Brendan O'Connor (Aqua-Fact Ltd, Galway), Dr Dáithí Ó hÓgáin and
Bairbre Ní Fhloinn (Department of Irish Folklore, University College Dublin)
and Richard Mills (Naturalist and photographer).
My Thanks to my wife Lailí, for having more patience than a wildlife film-maker
and to my son Cian, who by taking on more than his fair share of filming,
allowed me the extra time to devote to this book.*

This edition published in 1995 by
Tiger Books International PLC, Twickenham

ISBN 1-85501-729-6

First published in Great Britain in 1993 by Boxtree Limited

Text © Éamon de Buitléar 1993
The right of Éamon de Buitléar to be identified as Author of this Work
has been asserted by him in accordance with the
Copyright, Designs and Patents Act 1988.
1 3 5 7 9 10 8 6 4 2

Designed by Behram Kapadia
Format and typesetting by C & C Graphic Associates, Chesham
Printed in Italy by New Interlitho, Spa

A CIP catalogue entry for this book is available from the British Library

Contents

Introduction

*Ireland is a country of uneven surface and rather
mountainous. The soil is soft and watery, and there are many woods
and marshes. Even at the tops of high and steep mountains you
will find pools and swamps. Still there are, here and there,
some fine plains, but in comparison with the woods they are indeed
small. On the whole the land is low-lying on all sides and along
the coast; but further inland it rises up very high to many hills
and even high mountains. It is sandy rather than rocky,
not only on its circumference, but also
in the very interior.*

Giraldus Cambrensis
The History and Topography of Ireland, c.1200

*Right on the doorstep of the capital city
lies Dublin Bay, an internationally
important wetland filled with swirling flocks
of waders and wildfowl on migration from
breeding grounds in the arctic. This is where
many city people have their first real
experience of wildlife.*

Whenever I return home after a period overseas, I am reminded of the small size of the island on which I live and of the beauty and freshness of its wild countryside. I have used Ireland's landscapes as a back-drop in so many films in which the animals have been the actors that whenever I revisit those locations, I see them again as part of a story in which a particular mammal or bird has been the main performer.

The masses of colourful spring flowers in the old-fashioned uncut meadows along the banks of the River Shannon become part of the corncrake adventure; Dublin Bay, with its great flocks of winter wading birds wheeling over the mud flats, is an episode in the story of migration; the coast of Clare with schools of dolphins cutting through ocean waves is a scene from an underwater saga; the Killarney Mountains during the autumn, with the bellowing of native red stags, remain in the memory as a sequence from a tale about ancient Ireland; and the magical Loch Derravaragh in County Westmeath, resounding to the calls of migratory

whooper swans, will always be for me a part of that wonderful legend about the four children of King Lir, who on that very lake were put under a spell by their jealous stepmother and turned into wild swans.

Although parts of the Irish countryside may give the impression of having remained unchanged down through the ages, there is nowhere that has escaped the human imprint on the landscape. The great variety and mixture of habitats are features which I find attractive and which in some respects make up for the relatively small number of native plant and animal species found on the island. The land has an untailored look, and it is obvious from the miles of ungroomed hedgerows surrounding the patchwork of fields and farms that the country has escaped some of the worst impacts of post-war agricultural development.

The first people to reach Ireland arrived comparatively late, about 8,000 years ago, and when the first cattle arrived 3,000 years later there began a systematic conversion of ancient forest to farmland. Those early settlers

The typical rural landscape in lowland Ireland today is dominated by a patchwork of fields divided by hedges or stone walls. Similar fieldscapes were created by the first Irish farmers at least 5,000 years ago on the west coast and have been preserved beneath the blanket bog. The circular mound or rath in the centre of the picture, is the remains of a pre-christian settlement.

Rough grassland and coastal dunes are the main habitats of the skylark which nests on the ground and advertizes its territory by hovering in the air and delivering a continuous stream of musical notes.

established a highly organized society, and some of their extensive field systems are still visible in the west of Ireland, where the later blanket bogs are being stripped away.

Even today, farming has the greatest single influence on the shape of the countryside, from the small hay meadows of the north-west to the intensive cereal fields of the south-east. But increasingly, with each passing year, Ireland's farming folk are leaving the land, moving to urban areas or overseas in search of a livelihood, and the countryside is being turned over to a whole variety of new uses from forestry to golf courses. Whether the more sensitive forms of wildlife can survive these rapid changes remains to be seen, but thankfully there are still many quiet places off the beaten track where nature changes little from year to year.

A climate which includes high rainfall, strong winds and fast-changing weather systems sometimes results in the island experiencing all four seasons of the year on the same day, but foreign visitors often find this a pleasant change from endless days of monotonous sunshine in other parts of the world. As a film-maker, my defence of the weather would be that Ireland's magic fairylands, the peat bogs, would not exist were it not for the heavens being so generous with their share of rain. Nor would we have the countless picturesque lakes and rivers, nor the lush green vegetation for which the country is so famous.

The countryside and its wildlife have left their mark on Irish culture. Place-names, music and folklore are often linked with certain animals or plants: Foxfield, Salmon Leap, Birdhill, The Raven's Glen and Eagle's Rock are well-known places. Many traditional dance tunes seem also to owe their inspiration to the activities of some bird or mammal: 'The Hare in the Corn', 'The Blackbird', 'The Lark on the Strand', 'The Cuckoo's Nest' and 'The Fox Chase' are titles familiar to those who listen to Irish music.

> *Tá an chuach 's an smólach ag freagairt a chéile ann,*
>> *Tá an londubh 's an ceirseach ar gur, os a gcómhair,*
> *An gúld-finse, 'n creabhar, 's an linnet i gcage ann*
>> *An naosgach ag léimnigh, a's an eala ó'n Róimh.*
> *An t-iorlach as Acaill 's an fiach dubh ó'n gCéis ann,*
>> *An seabhac as Loch Éirne 's an fhuiseóg ó'n mhóin.*
> *'S dá mbeitheá ann ar maidin roimh éirí na gréine,*
>> *Go gloisfeá gach éan aca ag seinm san "ngróbh".*

Véarsa as Cill Aodain nó Condae Mhuigheo le Antoine O Raifteri

> There is the cuckoo and the thrush answering each other there
>> The blackbird and the ceirseach hatching over against them
> The goldfinch, the woodcock, and the linnet in a cage there,
>> The snipe leaping up, and the swan from Rome,
> The eagle out of Achill and the raven out of Kesh Corran,
>> The falcon from Loch Erne and the lark from the bog,
> And if you were to be there in the morning before rise of sun,
>> Sure you would hear every bird of them a-singing in the grove.

A translation by Douglas Hyde of a verse from the Irish song 'Killeaden or County Mayo', by the nineteenth-century blind poet Anthony O'Raftery

1

OCEAN AND SEA

Bhí trúir iascairí ann fadó, bhí currach acu agus ní leigeadh siad aoinne leo ach iad féin triúr, agus bhíodh a gcuid bídh agus ádhbhar tine mhóna acu. Aon lá amháin bhí siad amuigh ar an bhfairrge mhóir agus bhí siad tamall maith ó thalamh. Bhreathnuigh fear acu uaidh agus chonnaic sé rud mar a bheadh oileán. Ghreamuigh siad an churrach de le ceann de na dorugha agus ansin las siad tine. Shiubhail siad thart air ansin agus facthas dóibh go mba é an t-oileán ba deise ar thalamh an domhain é ach nach raibh aon dath féir ann. Dith siad an dinnéar agus nuair a bhí sé ithte acu shuidh siad síos go ciúin ag déanamh bolg le gréin. I gcionn tamaill niorbh fhada uatha ná gur airigh siad an t-oileán ag imeacht fútha agus déirigh siad suas go tapaidh. Cuaidh siad isteach ins an currach ar an bpointe agus is beag nar thug an míol mór go tóin iad ag imeacht dhó.

Three men were out at sea in their currach. They had their usual supply of food and peat with them. Away in the distance they saw something that looked like an island. When they reached it they tied the currach to one of the fins. They lit a fire and walked around. They thought it was the most beautiful island they had ever seen but there was no grass on it. When they had eaten their dinner they sat down to sunbathe. Before long they noticed that the island was moving. They immediately got into their currach and realized the island was in fact a big whale. The whale almost sunk their boat as he swam away. They fished all day and caught a lot of mackerel and then went home.

Department of Irish Folklore,
University College Dublin

Traditional Galway hookers racing home. These sailing craft have plied the waters of Galway Bay for centuries carrying goods around the coastal communities of Connemara. They were also used to bring turf (peat) to the Aran Islands and the Burren which had no fuel resources of their own. There has been a recent resurgence of interest in the hookers and many have been rebuilt. Their dramatic dark sails add a romantic touch to the western seascape.

Hauling lobster pots from a currach, the traditional small craft of the west coast. The boat is made of tar-covered canvas stretched over a framework of wooden laths. The sharp pointed bow is raised out of the water to slice through the Atlantic waves. These boats are still used on the west coast of Ireland.

One of the many exciting journeys that I have made was an underwater expedition with a group of marine biologists around the limestone coast of the Burren in County Clare. When calm weather prevails and conditions are right, these western coasts of Ireland are among the best in Europe for diving. The waters are unpolluted and the spectacular underwater scenery stretches for miles along the coast. As we swam above the curious fissured limestone pavements south of Black Head, we could see that every hollow and crack was filled with purple sea urchins. These spiky cousins of the starfish are much in demand on the French market, and this has led to their decline in areas where they are accessible to both tourists and commercial fishermen. Near the headland, we were treated to an eye-level view of a school of bottle-nosed dolphins ploughing through the water as they chased a shoal of mackerel. A curious grey seal watched us for only a short while before deciding it was safer to avoid these strange bubbling creatures altogether. Some weeks later, when I revisited the area and stood looking out over the bay where we had been diving, I wondered what my reaction would have been that day to the two gigantic and formidable killer whales which I could now see cruising along the coast!

Viewed from space, Ireland is perched like a boulder on top of a cliff, near the edge of the European continental shelf. Out beyond the west coast a wide shelf of sea bed slopes down gently to a depth of around 1,600ft (500m) and then drops away steeply into the pitch darkness to 8,125ft (2,500m) and the true Atlantic Ocean. In the 1880s and 1890s there were a number of expeditions, mostly sponsored by the Royal Irish Academy, to dredge and trawl the deep ocean floor off the west coast of Ireland. Amongst the crew on many of these trips was the famous naturalist Robert Lloyd Praeger, who in his autobiography *The Way That I Went* (1937) tells of his amazement at the variety of life brought up by the trawl from the sea floor a mile or more below the surface. 'There were great sea slugs, red and green; beautiful corals, numerous sea urchins with long slender spines; a great variety of starfishes of many shapes and of all colours, strange fishes and many other life forms.' He marvelled at the array of colours – 'purple, scarlet, orange, brilliant green were all there' – and at what might be the use of such colour in absolute darkness. Many of the specimens described by these expeditions were new to science at that time and, despite the technology now available to us, their deep ocean habitats remain as remote today as they were a century ago.

The underwater cliff which marks the edge of the European land mass produces an upwelling of ocean water, like the wind currents up the face of a land cliff. The edge of the shelf, which comes as close as 37 miles (60 km) to the County Mayo coastline, is the site for mixing of nutrients from the deep with light from the sun and a consequent explosion in productivity. Here on the open ocean, out of sight of land, are schools of whales and large feeding flocks of sea birds, unseen except by deep-sea fishermen and passengers on transatlantic ships. While the floating way of life suits the great whales, among the largest forms of wildlife on earth, it is also used by some of the smallest. The basis of all food chains in the ocean is the plankton, a soup of microscopic life-forms drifting at the mercy of the winds and currents. These tiny, often transparent specks of life are classified

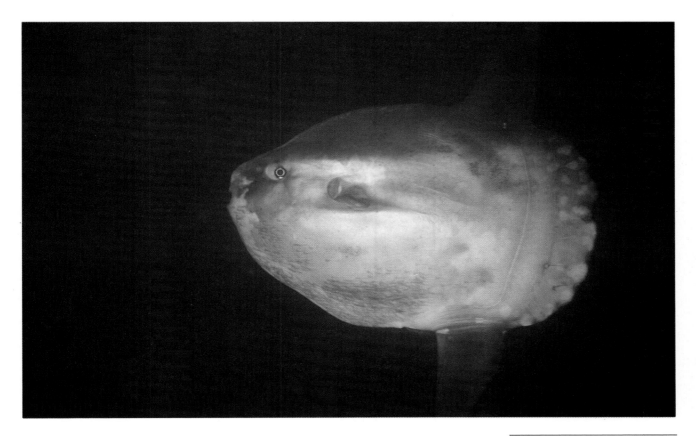

by marine scientists as either animals (zooplankton) or plants (phytoplankton). The plants are mainly single-celled organisms called diatoms, which, like the more familiar land and freshwater plants, are dependent on energy from the sun's rays to reproduce. To get enough light. these tiny plants must stay near the top of the ocean, and their minute size gives them a large surface area in relation to volume. This factor prevents them from sinking and is the key to their survival, for they must absorb all the mineral salts which they need for growth through the cell surface from the sea water. It is hard to imagine that such tiny plants are able to support the teeming animal life of the oceans, from vast fish shoals to schools of whales, but it is estimated that the sea produces a greater quantity of plant life than the same area of tropical forest.

Feeding on this plant soup is the floating animal life (zooplankton) of the ocean, which is more diverse than any animal community on land, despite the small size of each individual. Shrimp-like creatures, mostly no larger than a pinhead, make up the bulk of zooplankton, and may spend their entire life cycle floating at the surface. Others are the larval forms of bottom-dwelling worms, crabs or shellfish which release millions of eggs to the mercy of the water in the hope that a few will survive long enough to disperse over a wide area before they return to the sea bed as adults. Countless types of miniature jellyfish, some large enough to be seen with the naked eye, swim with pulsating rhythms through the water, although they, too, are carried along by the currents. The most important current in the North Atlantic Ocean is the Gulf Stream, which flows like a river from

The impressive sunfish appears in Irish waters each summer carried along by the North Atlantic Drift. It moves north from tropical waters carrying a full load of external parasites as passengers. It is thought to feed on jellyfish and occasionally turns side upwards to reach these animals floating on the surface.

the Caribbean Sea across thousands of miles of open ocean to warm the western coastal waters of Ireland. Carried along on this warm ocean current are larger members of the plankton such as the colonial hydrozoan *Velella*. I have often found the bluish, oval-shaped discs of these remarkable animals washed up on beaches in south-west Ireland and I can see just why fishermen have called the species the by-the-wind-sailor. Each one has a triangular fin, set diagonally across the body, just like the sail on a yacht. This projects above the surface of the water and allows the animal to be driven by the winds from the tropical waters where they breed. Pursuing them in the Gulf Stream are large predators such as the sunfish, a huge, round-bodied fish which can reach a length of up to 13ft (4m). They are seen by fishermen on the south-west coast of Ireland every summer, often floating on their sides. This habit of basking on the surface made the sunfish an easy target at a time when it was hunted with harpoons. The sunfish is also known as the floating motel, because of the variety and number of parasitic guests which take advantage of its slow movements to hitch a free lift on an ocean voyage.

Occasionally the nets or ropes of fishing gear become a trap for marine turtles which migrate through the waters of the continental shelf every year. I was once visiting a small harbour in west Galway when one of these magnificent creatures was brought ashore, towed alongside a small fishing boat. It resembled an upturned currach, one of the traditional black-tarred rowing boats which still ply between the islands and bays of this well-populated coastline. The news of this 'monster from the deep' soon spread among the inhabitants and most of the local population turned out to view the unfortunate leathery turtle which had by this time been towed out on to the slipway. It was over 6ft (nearly 2m) in length and must have weighed several tons with a leather-like 'shell' stretched across the ribs which ran from head to tail. More systematic reporting of these marine reptiles in recent years has shown that the leathery turtle is the commonest species found in Irish waters. Being air-breathing animals they can easily drown if trapped in fishing gear, and a campaign has been mounted to persuade fishermen to release any trapped turtles at sea where they belong. Other smaller species such as Ridley's turtle are occasionally found stranded on west coast beaches. They probably become weak if unable to catch enough of their staple food, jellyfish, in colder northern waters. Several of these tropical reptiles have been taken alive to the marine aquaria in Portaferry, County Down, and Bray, County Wicklow, from where they were flown back to their Caribbean home amidst a fanfare of publicity.

Ireland lies at a crossroads in the marine world. As well as the Gulf Stream from across the Atlantic, warm water flows northwards along the edge of the continental shelf carrying with it a planktonic community which originates in the salty waters of the Mediterranean. This 'Lusitanian' fauna appears at the surface on the coasts of south, south-west and west Ireland, and is represented by creatures such as the crayfish, red deadman's fingers and the trumpet anemone. To the north of Ireland the marine life includes Arctic-Boreal animals like the stonecrab. The warm water enters the semi-enclosed Irish Sea between County Wexford and south Wales, and the colder northern current flows south between County Antrim and south-

Top Left: Starfish (Henricia oculata) *and sea anemone* (Sagartia elegans) *off Clare Island, County Mayo. Both animals are characteristic of exposed rocky shores where there is strong wave action and water movement. In the clear waters of the west coast these animals tend to be more brightly coloured.*

Bottom Left: Leathery turtle on a pier at Rosbeg, County Donegal. Each year many of these marine reptiles are seen in Irish waters and some become entangled in fishing gear and drown. Fishermen are encouraged to release them at sea rather than bringing them ashore.

Despite its impressive size, the basking shark is quite slow-moving and harmless. It swims near the surface with its huge mouth wide open sieving plankton from the seawater. Hundreds of these fish were hunted in western Ireland as the oil from their livers was a valuable fuel but the population collapsed in the mid-twentieth century.

west Scotland. The two currents meet in a zone of frontal mixing across the north Irish Sea which brings rich plankton swarms to the surface, attracting huge basking sharks. At up to 42ft (13m) in length, these are the largest fish in Irish waters. The sight of a triangular dorsal fin cutting through the coastal waters is enough to send alarm signals through the ranks of onlookers, but in fact these massive fish are completely harmless. As they swim about, their enormous gaping mouths sieve the plankton soup from the sea and expel the water through huge gills or slits in the side of the neck. I find it most interesting to listen to the old Aran fishermen discussing the marine life around the islands and to hear them reminisce about the days when they were young. One islander told me that on many occasions all the currachs would have to head back for the shore, because the basking sharks were so numerous in the bay that the fishermen feared their boats would be overturned.

As the sharks are quite slow-moving, it is possible for scuba divers to swim alongside them. Improvements in modern scuba diving gear have now allowed scientists to explore the sea bed down to a depth of about 162ft (50m). Marine zoologists from University College, Galway, have made full use of this kind of technology to carry out a long and valuable programme of research along the west coast. Of particular interest for some of the study programmes is the wide bay around Cill Chiaráin in Connemara. In this area the sea floor is covered in masses of *Lithothamnion*, often referred to in Ireland as coral. When I went to film the marine life on that part of the coast for the first time, it was at the invitation of Dr Brendan Keegan of UCG,

Above: Coral Strand (An Dóilín), *Carraroe, County Galway. These unique white beaches in Connemara are made not of coral but of fragments of a calcareous algae known as maerl which grows in the clear inshore waters and is washed ashore in winter storms.*

Left: Maerl (Lithothamnion) *is an algae which forms large underwater beds at various locations off the west coast. The beds are occasionally found near the low tide mark but in clear water may reach down to about 50ft (15m). As with tropical coral reefs the maerl beds provide shelter for many other animals including molluscs, sea cucumbers and sea urchins.*

Top: The sea cucumber (Neopentadactyla mixta) *lives with part of its body buried in coarse gravel on the seabed while it waves a crown of soft feathery arms around to catch plankton in the water. A relative of the starfish, it has ten large arms and five rows of tube feet on the body.*

Middle: The Sea anemone secures itself to rocks by means of its adhesive sucker-like disc.

Bottom: Featherstars (Antedon bifida) *are normally attached to rocky surfaces but here they have moved onto a stem of seaweed or kelp in order to reach up clear of the seabed into the plankton. These relatives of starfish cling onto the kelp with little feet (cirri) which they use to move about.*

who was leading a team of diving biologists on one of their many underwater expeditions in the region. It was very early morning when we dived from the research vessel and descended to a depth of about 65ft (20m). The visibility was clear as we landed on what looked like a vast under-sea desert of rough, pinkish, gravelly material, all of which had been spectacularly formed into hollows and small hillocks by the ocean currents. This coral-like substance, which stretched away into the distance as far as the eye could see, is an unattached calcified seaweed which forms the material for several beaches in Connemara. Where it lies along the shoreline in places such as the Coral Strand (An Doilín) at Carraroe, it is of a much brighter colour as a result of bleaching by the sun. The most exciting part of this panoramic view, however, was not the sea floor itself but the carpet of strange creatures that appeared to be growing out of it. The scene resembled a vast underwater garden of beautiful exotic flowers, quite unlike anything I had ever seen before. They were not plants but animals, and there were acres of them, pale-coloured sea cucumbers (*Neopentadactyla mixta*) swaying to and fro as they reacted to the strong tide flowing across the ocean bed. On looking closer, I could see that the cucumbers were not just waving as a result of the currents, they were using their flower-like limbs in a dancing movement to collect food from just above the surface of the sea floor. This was feeding time for the sea cucumbers, and the biologists had timed their dive to coincide with these activities. In about three hours these animals would disappear back into their underground burrows, leaving the sea floor looking empty and bare. They seem to react to changes in water temperature, which may be one of the reasons why this species of sea cucumber remains hidden altogether during the winter months.

The animal communities which live on the bed of the Irish Sea reflect the range of bottom sediments and the degree of exposure. During the last Ice Age, large quantities of boulders, gravel and sand were dumped by glaciers in the Irish Sea basin, and with rising sea levels these have been sorted and worked by tides and marine currents. On each rising tide the sea rushes into Strangford Lough, a large sea inlet in County Down, through a deep and rocky channel known as the Narrows. It then slows down to fill the increasingly shallow, island-studded inlet which stretches away for 15 miles (24km) to the north. Every day millions of cubic metres of water pass in and out of the Lough carrying a rich mixture of planktonic food from the Irish Sea. The daily surge of the tide through the Narrows can reach speeds of up to 7 knots, so strong that the powerful car-ferry crossing between the villages of Strangford and Portaferry is forced to move with a crab-like motion across the current. Standing on the deck of the ferry it is easy to appreciate the speed of the water as swimming birds such as cormorants and gulls go racing by and are spun around in whirlpools caused by drag on the bedrock. Virtually all the animal communities from the bed of the Irish Sea are found together within Strangford Lough because it contains almost the full range of sub-littoral habitats. The strong currents of the Narrows scour the bedrock and large boulders where only a few species of brightly coloured sponges and encrusting soft corals are able to hang on. Between the boulders masses of tiny tubes of the colonial hydroid *Turbellaria* reach up to feed in the currents. As the speed of the tides decreases further north, sediments including gravels and coarse sands form the bottom of the Lough. All surfaces of the sand are covered with a living tangle of arms of the common brittlestar (*Ophiothrix)*, which stretches as far as the eye can see in the murky light. In the central parts of the Lough, where slower currents flow over mud and shell debris, there is yet another rich community dominated by the horse mussel (*Modiolus)*, individuals of which may be several decades old. Like a tropical coral reef, the dense beds of mussels provide shelter for a huge array of other marine animals like sea cucumbers, tube worms, sea squirts and variegated scallops. The commercial value of scallops has led to extensive bottom-trawling causing destruction of large parts of the horse mussel beds. The waters which pass over these and many other sea-bed communities in Strangford Lough are filled with enormous shoals of fish for which the Lough is especially important as a spawning area. Throughout the summer huge numbers of pencil-thin silvery fish can be seen near the surface as they reflect the sunlight like a million tiny mirrors. These

are sand eels, which pour into the Lough to spawn in the sand banks near low-water mark.

Sand eels were once a valued seasonal food item for some of the coastal communities around the northern part of Ireland. Large gatherings of local people were common at the lowest spring tides near the mouth of coastal bays such as Mulroy Bay, County Donegal. Using shovels and rakes and specially blunted sickles, they would dig for the fish in the soft sands. Sand eels were used as bait for long-line fishing, and the surplus catch was salted and dried for the hungry months before the potatoes and corn were harvested. At Dundrum Bay, not far from Strangford Lough, I have tried digging sand eels myself and found that it requires some considerable skill to whip the slippery fish from the sand into a bucket before they escape. For many of the larger animals of Strangford and other sea loughs and bays around the Irish coast, sand eels are an essential part of the summer diet. Common seals inhabit these sheltered waters from County Down around

Atlantic breakers produce a mass of white foam on Clogher Beach near Dún Chaoin, County Kerry. In the distance is the distinctive outline of Inis Tuaisceart, one of the Blasket Islands.

the west coast and as far south as Bantry Bay in west Cork. They prefer to feed in the narrow channels near the mouth of the bays where the fish are confined and easier to chase. At low tide they haul themselves out of the water on to weed-covered rocks or sand banks to rest and digest their food. As they dry out in the sun, their coats change from dark to light grey and even to a creamy white. Seals are highly sociable mammals which prefer to live in groups, probably made up of related animals. On several occasions I have got close enough to photograph the interplay between the seals, which usually means crawling among weed-covered rocks to avoid disturbing them. A few times I have been lucky enough to see the new-born pups in June or July, swimming close to their mothers or suckling in the weedy shallows. As the tide rises, covering the haul-out areas, the seals become more restless, constantly shifting position. They raise their heads and hind-flippers out of the water until, in silhouette, they resemble a pile of bananas. Then, one by one, they slide off into deeper water to resume their daily

feeding routine. In the autumn, common seals haul out in greatest numbers when they moult their furry coats. At this time there is much excited activity among the herd and some seals perform dolphin-like leaps jumping clear of the water.

The salmon which migrate along the west coast of Ireland in summer are forced to run a gauntlet of drift nets. Huge numbers are caught (the majority illegally), and only a minority make the ultimate journey to spawn in their natal rivers. The thrashing fish, caught fast in the meshes of monofilament nylon, provide an irresistible feast for Atlantic grey seals. *Rón*, the Irish name for the seals, appears in the names of many west-coast rocks and islands such as Roaninish in County Donegal. I have often seen these magnificent animals around Great Blasket Island, off the tip of the Dingle peninsula in County Kerry. The White Strand *(An Trá Bhán)*, which stretches out beneath the long-deserted village, is the haul-out place for one of Ireland's largest herds of grey seals. The white-coated pups are born in

The Great Blasket Island (An Blascaod Mór), County Kerry (on the right) has been compared to 'a great whale surrounded by her young'. These, the most westerly group of islands in Ireland, had a thriving community until they were finally evacuated to the mainland in 1953. Today the islands are inhabited only by seabirds, seals and sheep.

The grey seal is the larger of the two seal species found in Ireland and mainly inhabits the rocky headlands and islands of the Atlantic coast. The white-coated pups are born in autumn on remote beaches and caves and remain on land for up to three weeks after which they are abandoned by the female. Eventually, hunger forces the seal pup to take to the sea where it soon learns to fend for itself.

autumn and after three weeks of suckling on the beach they are deserted by the mother. Hunger eventually drives them down to the water in search of food, and they soon learn to fend for themselves in the ocean where they will spend the rest of their lives. In the last century seals were hunted here by the islanders at great risk to their own lives. Tomás Ó Criomthain, in his famous book *An tOileánach* (*The Islandman*), wrote of how the men would swim into caves after the adult seals. Each carried a candle and matches under his cap and a club under his arm. Having dispatched the seals in near-darkness, they tied them to long ropes to be dragged out by others waiting at the cave mouth. Both the skin and the meat were a great resource for the islanders, especially in times of hardship. Grey seals were widely hunted in many other parts of the Irish coast including north-west Mayo, where another group of remote islands, the Inishkeas, is now the other main centre of the population. While on a visit to the ruined village on Inishkea North, I walked around the rocky shoreline where I finally reached a narrow neck of land separating a rocky peninsula from the rest of the island. Here I lay low and crept forward on hands and knees until I was close enough to hear the grunting and moaning of up to 100 grey seals hauled out on the edge of a weed-filled creek. Such impressive sights have only become possible since these islands were deserted in the 1930s and hunting pressure on the seals was relaxed. There was a belief along some parts of the coast that seals were people of the sea, who could cast aside their skins at certain times and regain human shape. Anybody who has heard the enchanting chorus of sounds created by these animals could well imagine how such stories originated. It was even said of particular families that they were related to seals, and that when these people passed on they made their homes in the sea. The story of the man who married a seal-person is well known. The husband is said to have hidden the woman's outer garment, without which she could not go back to her ocean environment. When the wife eventually discovered her seal skin, she donned it and immediately made her way back to the sea, never to return again.

One of the most exciting encounters I have had with marine mammals was while filming a dolphin near the mouth of Dingle Harbour. This wild bottle-nosed dolphin made its first appearance here in 1983 and seemed to like the attentions of curious humans so much that it stayed on for many years. Such has been the fame of the Dingle Dolphin that a local tourist industry has built up around it, with thousands of holiday-makers each summer paying for a boat-ride around the natural harbour and the privilege of a few glimpses of this wild creature from the sea. The dolphin reacts in a specially friendly manner to scuba divers and will even allow those in whom it has confidence to touch and stroke it. Such trust of humans is rare in wild animals, which usually have good reason to be afraid of our species. The west and south-west coasts of Ireland are among the best places in Europe to see dolphins in the wild, and I have a number of favourite viewpoints. The Shannon Estuary, almost 50 miles (80km) in length, is like a wide funnel opening up to the rolling swell from the Atlantic. On its northern side the long limestone arm of Loop Head reaches out to the ocean, and from the old lighthouse on the point I have seen dozens of bottle-nosed dolphins passing in and out of the estuary. They probably drive shoals of fish into the narrow waters, just like sheepdogs working together to drive a herd of sheep through a gate. Further north on the coast of County Clare, I have stood on the beach at Fanore and watched porpoises and dolphins plying backwards and forwards in the sound between the Aran Islands and the mainland. In County Mayo schools of dolphins are frequently seen in summer in Clew Bay and from the Mullet Peninsula in the extreme north-west of the county. I remember once, on a boat trip through Broadhaven, the wide inlet between the peninsula and the mainland, being surrounded by a group of the rare Risso's dolphin, which has a rounded bulging head instead of the familiar beak of other dolphins, and pale grey flanks scarred with numerous scrape marks, the origin of which is unknown.

Most recorded strandings of the larger whales in Ireland are from the south and west coasts which suggests that significant numbers of these mammals pass along the continental shelf in their annual migrations. This was well known to the Norwegian whalers of the early twentieth century, who had by then already over-exploited the whale stocks in their own waters and begun to move on to fresh pastures. In 1908, the Arranmore Whaling Company set up a whaling station on the islands of Inishkea where the rusting metal remains of machinery used by the whalers are still visible today on the boulder beach. Between 1908 and 1913 some 387 great whales were caught by the Arranmore Whaling Company. Most were fin whales but there were also significant numbers of sei, right, sperm and blue whales. The latter species, the largest of all marine mammals, can reach over 90ft (up to 30m) in length, or the size of a fishing trawler. When, in 1914, the

The large holdfasts of brown seaweeds are like the anchors of ships. The blade of this kelp (Saccorhiza polyschides), here pictured at St John's Point, County Donegal, has broken off in winter storms and is deposited on the shoreline. The following year an entirely new blade will grow to replace it.

outbreak of war put an end to whaling from Ireland, over-exploitation had already made some of these giant animals a rare sight in Irish waters. Occasionally, however, there are much publicized strandings of smaller whales, and in 1977 a lone killer whale stayed for a number of days in the mouth of the River Foyle, in full view of the citizens of Derry. After feeding on the late run of salmon up the river, he made his way back to sea off the north coast of Donegal.

The most common habitat on the Irish coast is a low rocky shore covered with a blanket of brown seaweeds. At the very limit of the low tide great waving forests of kelp with long, strap-like fronds or leaves are revealed. These are favourite feeding grounds for otters, which are active by day on the west coast due to the lack of disturbance. Higher up the shore are various zones dominated by different brown seaweeds such as serrated wrack, bladder wrack, spiral wrack and channelled wrack. Slithering among the boulders at low tide, I have often noticed the constant background noise of water trickling from the countless rock pools. Here there is an abundance of seashore life which is covered with a film of water even at low tide. Barnacles and mussels cling tightly to the rock surface and feed from the plankton which swirls over them with each rising tide. Limpets and periwinkles move about, grazing on the algae and other plant life attached to the rocks. Turning over a large rock from a pool, I find it covered with a mass of encrusting forms including sponges, sea mats and the sea anemones which send out a jet of water when touched. Small fish and shrimps swim among the colourful red, brown and green seaweeds in the lower rock pools, and the hermit crab, with its adopted shell, shuffles about in search of food. In rock pools in Donegal, Sligo, Galway and Clare, the purple sea urchin lives in large colonies and actually dissolves the limestone rock beneath it, forming millions of tiny depressions.

On one occasion I filmed a pair of otters in the picturesque area of Killary Harbour. It was a bitterly cold November morning with a sharp northerly wind blowing, and I lay hidden among some stones close to the edge of the sea. It had occurred to me several times that morning that lying motionless like this on an exposed beach in the middle of winter was not the best way of keeping warm during harsh weather! The otters I had spotted were busy fishing about 100ft (30m) out from the shore and up-wind of my position. I knew that if they were to come any closer I would have to be extremely cautious. The stones gave me very little cover, and if these shy animals sense a human nearby they will quickly disappear. Experience has taught me that the otter's senses of smell and hearing are extremely acute and that, although its eyesight is not by any means as sharp as its nose and ears, any movement on my part at this range would cause the pair immediate alarm. I could clearly hear the otters whistling whenever they surfaced. These sound signals enable otters to keep in touch when they lose sight of one another, especially when the sea is rough, as it was on that particular morning. Both otters were busy, and almost every dive brought results in the way of small fish. I knew that this activity would continue for several hours. An agile, energetic animal which spends most of its time in a cold, wet environment requires a lot of food to build up its reserves. The otters were too far away for me to identify their catch, but I took it to be mostly the eel-like butterfish, one of their favourite foods – an efficient operator like the otter finds little difficulty in locating their hiding places under stones on the sea floor. The wintry conditions and rough water did not seem to pose any problems for the otters, and every time one of these capable anglers surfaced with a fish it immediately began chewing vigorously and holding on to its prey with its front paws. The otters were working the tide and gradually making their way down-wind, to a position which would bring them almost directly opposite to the point on the shore where I was doing my best to remain invisible.

What I had been hoping for all along eventually happened: one of the otters caught a very large fish which it could not possibly manage to control or eat out at sea. It immediately began to swim with its struggling victim, straight to the shoreline and almost directly towards me! Now the question was, would the otter see what it regarded as its arch-enemy waiting for it on the beach as it headed towards the shore? For once the piercing northerly wind was doing me a favour. It whipped the tide and forced the otter to concentrate on getting its wriggling quarry to dry land. The mouthful of fish was also partly blocking its view as it battled with the Atlantic swell. It all took a lot of effort and hard work, and as the otter pulled its slippery prize on to the kelp-covered beach it began feeding ravenously on it. The fish was by now partly visible, and I took it to be an eelpout a foot (30cm) or so in length. The activity now taking place on the shore was no more than about 20ft (7m) from where this half-frozen film-maker was focusing his lens.

In western Ireland the heron *(an corr riasc)* is most commonly seen stalking fish and crabs in the weedy shallows and among the rock pools at low tide. In Connemara, herons nest in colonies on wooded islands in the lakes which speckle the blanket bog, but they feed almost exclusively around the long, indented coastline and even roost on islands and headlands at high tide until their feeding grounds are exposed again. The grey crow has learned that living close to a heronry can have its rewards. I have often watched a pair from a hide, waiting for feeding time at a heron's nest. As soon as the adult heron arrived they would mob it and tantalize it relentlessly, until the pestered bird was forced to disgorge the fish intended for the baby herons.

Wherever mussels grow on the rocks, oystercatchers are common predators, and the piles of broken mussel shells along the strandline are evidence of their work. Other waders, such as ringed plover, dunlin, turnstone and purple sandpiper, are widespread on the rocky shores of the Irish coast in winter. Several of these species prefer the weed-covered boulder beaches which offer them the greatest abundance and variety of invertebrate food. They seem oblivious to the presence of human onlookers as they move rapidly about catching the fast-moving insects.

The estuaries of Ireland are like precious stones on a necklace, linked together by the continuous line of the coast, but each one is individual in character. The extensive sand and mud flats which form the major habitat types in the estuaries are among the last surviving areas of wilderness in Ireland, largely unchanged since the end of the Ice Age. As wildlife habitats they are of immense importance, and their proximity to the major human settlements makes them very accessible. Perhaps the best-known estuaries in Ireland are those on which the major cities and their ports are built: Dublin Bay, Cork Harbour, Shannon Estuary, Galway Bay, Lough Foyle and Belfast Lough. Each has a multiplicity of functions, as shipping channels, fish nursery grounds, bait-digging sites and areas for shellfish cultivation, waste disposal and recreation, as well as wildlife habitats.

The multiple uses of Irish estuaries are well illustrated by Dublin Bay, which is the cradle of the capital city. Founded over 1,000 years ago at the mouth of the River Liffey, Dublin has grown up around the bay and has come to depend on it. Throughout the centuries sections of salt marsh and mud flat around the river mouth, now largely occupied by the city docks and modern port, were surrounded by wooden embankments, drained and cultivated to feed the growing human population. The collection of shellfish from the sand at low tide reached a peak in the late nineteenth century when up to seventy people were engaged in this activity and over 80 tonnes of cockles were marketed annually. Indeed, this figure is probably a gross underestimate of the harvest, as the bulk of the cockles was taken by local people for home consumption or for sale from street barrows. But the city sewers emptied into the river and thence to the estuary and, with the growing urban population, Dublin Bay became grossly polluted in the early years of the twentieth century. There is strong evidence linking the high incidence of typhoid in the city to the eating of contaminated shellfish, before the cockle fishery collapsed.

Constant siltation caused the shipping channels to become blocked, and

eventually it became necessary to build retaining walls at the mouth of the River Liffey. The completion of the Great South Wall and the Bull Wall brought a change in tidal circulation in Dublin Bay, and within a few years sand banks began to build up eventually forming North Bull Island, a sand-dune system about 3 miles (3.8km) in length. Centuries of human sewage entering Dublin Bay had produced an organic ooze of soft mud in the inner reaches where the tidal currents are weakest, and the growth of North Bull Island isolated a large sheltered lagoon from the main part of the bay. This lagoon contains enormous quantities of worms, crustaceans, bivalve molluscs and especially the tiny gastropod *Hydrobia*.

Many Irish estuaries also have substantial banks of mussels growing attached to rocks, to gravel or to one another. On the east side of Lough Foyle in County Derry the mussel beds are so extensive that they act as a trap for the tide and force it to deposit fine silt all along the shore. The high density of lugworms below the surface of this mud is revealed by the large number of worm casts on the surface. All these invertebrates comprise the staple diet of the waders which are such important visitors to Irish estuaries.

As the summer evenings draw in and the days begin to shorten, the vast empty expanses of Irish estuaries take on a new urgency. Growing flocks of waders such as curlew begin to assemble with their young from the breeding season just completed. They have moved down from their breeding grounds in the high moorlands of Ireland, Scotland and Scandinavia to spend the autumn months fattening up on the abundant supplies of shellfish and lugworms before moving on further south. As the tide creeps in across the

Wader roost at Dunkettle, Cork. As the tide covers their feeding areas, waders are forced to take refuge on sand banks, saltmarsh and on artificial structures such as piers and embankments. Here they form mixed species groups with each bird jostling with its neighbours for the best position in the roost.

Curlew – the largest of the waders on the Irish coast and the one with the longest bill. It feeds by probing deep in the mud and twisting its head so that the curved bill makes a sweep below the surface to detect buried food items such as lugworms, by touch.

bay, they are forced up into the salt marsh near the high-tide mark where the last purple flowers of the sea aster are still in bloom. The lonely cries of the curlew carry far across the flat open landscape as they gather in tight flocks to preen and rest until the tide retreats to lay bare their feeding grounds again. All along the south coast of Ireland from Wexford to Cork, a chain of small estuaries begins to fill with birds including internationally important numbers of black-tailed godwit from the Icelandic breeding grounds. Some of these birds are still in partial moult, and the russet colour of their breeding plumage catches the autumn sunlight as they feed intensively between the tides. In midwinter, when daylight hours are short, the lives of waders are controlled by the rise and fall of the tide and they even feed by moonlight if the tide is low.

In the north of Ireland the larger estuaries of Lough Foyle and Strangford Lough are the first landfall sites for the flocks of brent geese arriving in autumn from their staging grounds in Iceland. These small, handsome geese are from the light-bellied race which breeds in the Canadian high Arctic and winters almost exclusively in Ireland. They call constantly to one another as they settle in to graze on their preferred food, eel-grass, a marine flowering plant which grows in quantity in about a dozen Irish estuaries. This grass-like plant is most abundant in September and October, after which it dies back to form deep deposits on the strandline. To walk barefoot among these beds of eel-grass is a memorable experience as the sand surface is covered with a thin sheet of water even at low tide and the grass is soft and flowing. The vast eel-grass beds of Lough Foyle, Strangford Lough, Tralee Bay and

Castlemaine Harbour are a vital resource for the geese, and when they have exhausted the supply they begin to disperse around the coast to find other, less energy-rich foods such as green seaweeds for the rest of the winter.

As the daylight hours reach their shortest and the winter sunlight sends long shadows across the sands, the estuaries finally fill with birdlife. Vast wheeling flocks of waders such as dunlin, knot and godwit fill the skies at high tide as they search for a space to roost among the salt-marsh plants. The piping calls of the oystercatchers are ever more shrill as the competition for cockles or mussels becomes intense in the short, cold winter days. The calls of the waders are especially welcome in midwinter when most songbirds are silent. Fast-moving groups of whitish sanderlings hurtle backwards and forwards at the edge of the tide, picking up tiny crustaceans from the wet sand. Large rafts of wigeon swim in the muddy channels or range across the mud, grazing on green seaweeds. If a prolonged period of severe cold occurs in Britain or continental Europe, many of the migrant birds move west to Ireland with its milder, damper oceanic climate. In some years this results in large flocks of curlew, lapwing and golden plover moving into the estuaries in midwinter. The numbers of birds fluctuate from year to year, but each estuary has a limited carrying capacity mainly due to the available food resources. Eighteen Irish estuaries regularly hold internationally important numbers of waders or wildfowl (more than 10,000 ducks, geese or swans, more than 20,000 waders, or more than 1 per cent of the flyway population of any waterfowl species). These are the top sites and the most important links in the East Atlantic Flyway.

The problem for conservation of Irish estuaries is that they do not have the immediate scenic attractions of mountains, lakes or woodlands. Many of them are vast, flat and apparently empty places, which encourages the view that they are worthless wastelands just waiting to be filled in or 'reclaimed' from the sea. On many Irish estuaries there has already been substantial loss of salt marsh, and concrete embankments stretch for many miles around the shores of places such as the Fergus Estuary, County Clare, Lough Foyle, County Derry, and Wexford Harbour, cutting off the sea from the low-lying land around the coast. Port and industrial developments have taken over the upper parts of most estuaries which have a city or large town, and in some, such as Dublin Bay and Cork Harbour, there is pressure to take still more of the bay to create new roads. Disposal of untreated sewage to estuaries still continues in many urban areas such as Galway Bay, and this has made the harvesting of shellfish a dangerous and illegal practice. In some estuaries there are major municipal rubbish dumps as at Belfast Lough, County Down, Rogerstown Estuary, County Dublin, and Tramore Back Strand, County Waterford. This short-sighted method of waste disposal is not only unnecessary but is also permanently damaging the wildlife habitats in these estuaries. There is an urgent need for estuaries and shallow coastal areas to be treated as important and valuable natural resources, for sustainable uses such as mussel-growing to be encouraged, and damaging practices such as dumping halted. Damage to our coastal waters, with their magical sounds, wide skies and open vistas, is equivalent to robbing the jewels from the crown of this green island.

2

ISLAND
AND SHORE

*To the shores of boulders and pebbles the men take their straddled horses,
a basket on each side with ropes made of horse-hair attached.
High over the straddle they pile the seaweed and hold it together with
the ropes. And those hard Aran ponies of the Conamara strain pick their
way over the slippery, moss-covered flags, between large boulders
and pebbles that give way under pressure of hoof, with the
sureness of goats among the crags of a mountain.*

Thomas O'Flaherty,
Cliffmen of the West, 1935

*The rocks which form the cliffs on the Aran
Islands are similar to those of the Burren,
with horizontal beds of limestone and shale
falling sheer to the Atlantic Ocean. Seabirds
such as fulmars nest on the cliff ledges and sea
pinks thrive in the salt-laden winds.*

The otter is widespread in Ireland although not usually seen by day except in undisturbed areas such as remote parts of the west coast. An agile swimmer, it is at home both in freshwater and in the sea where it catches rock fish, eels and crabs. Otters often swim out to offshore islands where their distinctive footprints can be followed on sandy beaches.

One of my regular occupations when I am on the west coast is otter-watching. I have spent hours following the activities of these fascinating animals, along western shorelines as well as on various islands. Among my favourite haunts are some undisturbed bays in Mayo and Connemara, where otters are often active during daylight hours. The knowledge of local people is sometimes helpful, and I remember one farmer whom I met walking along a rocky beach. He described vividly where the otter had been and even pointed out a big boulder where the animal had regularly left its spraint as a signal to others of its kind. His last sighting of the otter had been about ten years previously, but when I examined the beach I found signs of one which had passed that way only a few hours before. Life still moves at a very leisurely pace in parts of Ireland, and folk memory goes back a long way! Indeed, it is probable that otters have been using this relatively undisturbed stretch of coastline since the end of the last Ice Age, and they will probably continue to do so for as long as their environment here is left intact.

With a total length of over 3,700 miles (6,000km) (excluding the countless islands), and a wide diversity of rock types and sediments, the coastline of Ireland has infinite variety of landscape and wildlife. The plants and animals below the waves remain mysteriously out of sight most of the time, but those which live above the shoreline are among our most familiar. The coastline is a zone of change between the habitats of land and sea and contains many highly productive ecosystems. In these areas animals and plants have evolved so that they are tolerant to varying degrees of exposure to salt spray or occasional flooding by the tide. Some of the animals, such as otters, spend only part of their lives on land and the remainder at sea – they are dependent on both. Ireland is shaped like a saucer, with a broad flat central plain and a ring of mountains round the edge. The rock types are extremely varied and their hardness and colour have a profound influence on the coastal scenery. In the north-east a sheet of basalt lies on top of the only chalk deposit in Ireland, giving the distinctive black and white cliffs of Rathlin Island, County Antrim. In County Clare, on the west coast, flat beds of limestone, sandstone and shale form a spectacular stepped landscape which is best exposed in the Burren region near Black Head. In West Kerry the folded beds of Old Red Sandstone are picked out in the setting sun over the Atlantic Ocean. In each of these coastal regions the land and sea have been readjusting to each other in varying degrees since the last Ice Age, over 10,000 years ago. Thus we find raised beaches in the north-east around County Antrim and drowned river valleys and peatlands below the present high-water mark in the south-west around Counties Kerry and Clare.

Superimposed on this tilting platform of diverse rock types are different degrees of exposure to wave energy. The north and west coasts are characterized by high wave-energy from the Atlantic Ocean producing spectacular cliffs, islands, rocky shores, storm beaches and the unique sandy machair grasslands. On the south and east coasts, the wave energy is lower and the coastal landscapes are softer, with many stretches of sand dunes, shingle and estuarine mud. Cliffs have formed around the Irish coastline where high wave-energy interacts with hard, resistant rock types. Not surprisingly, the highest, most spectacular cliffs are on the west coast with its numerous islands, but there are many lower cliffs on the north, east and especially the south coasts. Among the best-known places on the west coast are the Cliffs of Moher in County Clare, rising vertically 650ft (200m) from the sea and extending about 6 miles (10km) along the coast. They are formed of horizontal beds of Carboniferous sandstone and shale, and as a result their ledges have both a rich flora and a large colony of nesting sea birds. In contrast, the cliffs of Slieve League in County Donegal, which reach 1,950 ft (600 m) above sea level, are made of ancient Pre-Cambrian quartzite and gneiss which do not readily form suitable ledges for sea birds. However, their sheer height and north-facing exposure make them the habitat for an exciting range of Arctic–Alpine plants.

Of the island cliffs few can compare for starkness and beauty with the Skellig Rocks off County Kerry. These two isolated crags of Old Red Sandstone rise like volcanoes from the Atlantic. Once one of the most remote Early Christian monastic sites in Europe, they are now home in summer to one of Europe's largest gannet colonies. The islands of Ireland have always held a certain fascination for naturalists from the days of Robert Lloyd Praeger and the Survey of Clare Island, County Mayo (1911–15), to the present Bird Observatory on Cape Clear Island, County Cork. Perhaps this is as a result of the feeling of isolation from the rest of the world or the fact that an island has well-defined boundaries and a specific range of wildlife species. An ever-present feature of island life is the exposure to wind and salt spray. Few Irish islands can support significant tree cover, although on Clare Island there is a small area of birch woodland which has survived since Praeger's days in a sheltered eastern valley. Often the only cover is

The Cliffs of Moher are among the most impressive mainland cliffs in Ireland, extending for five miles (8km) along the coast of County Clare. The flat ledges of shale and flagstones hold a large colony of seabirds including kittiwakes, razorbills and guillemots. Far below, the Atlantic breakers smash against the foot of the cliffs.

provided by a few stunted bushes and trees growing around abandoned houses and gardens. On Cape Clear Island, many hedges are composed of exotic species such as *fuchsia* and *escallonia* giving the visitor an illusion of subtropical conditions. With the warming influence of the North Atlantic Drift, winter frosts are extremely rare on these west-coast islands, which means that some Mediterranean plants survive. On Cape Clear Island, three of these are annuals – chaffweed, yellow centaury and the rare hairy bird's foot trefoil. One of my favourite islands is the Great Saltee, off County

Wexford, which was farmed up until the 1940s but whose fields are now overrun with bracken and the old stone farmhouse deserted except for visiting birdwatchers who use it as a base to monitor the island's bird life.

A visit to an island like the Great Saltee is an experience for all the senses as the sounds and smells are as strong as the visual images. The clifftops and ledges take on a new vibrancy in early summer with the return of the nesting sea birds. Many of these birds spend the majority of their lives feeding far from land, returning briefly to their natal colony to rear their

The island of Great Saltee, off County Wexford has an important seabird colony with about 1,200 pairs of gannets breeding on the rugged southern cliffs. At the south-east corner of Ireland, the island is often the first landfall for spring migrants arriving from their African wintering grounds.

Above: Outside the nesting season the kittiwake ranges widely over the ocean. It comes to land only for breeding and builds its nest on the most sheer of cliff faces using its own droppings to cement the nest material to the rock. The black markings on the tips of the kittiwake's primary feathers give the impression that its wings were dipped in ink.

Right: Guillemots do not build a nest but lay their single egg on a narrow ledge and hold it in place with their feet. Before the young chicks are fully grown they 'parachute' down to the sea below where they continue to be fed by their parents until they learn to fish for themselves.

own young. Ireland has twenty-two species of breeding seabird, with a total of nearly 220,000 auks (guillemots, razorbills and puffins) and at least 224,000 pairs of the other species. This total does not include the huge, but virtually unknown, numbers of storm petrels which nest unseen in burrows and crevices in at least twenty-eight colonies around the Irish coast. The Irish colonies of Manx shearwater, storm petrel and gannet make up a sizeable part of the European populations of these birds. Almost every surface in a seabird colony is used as a breeding territory, including the roofs of buildings. The main habitats used are the rocky crevices and ledges of the cliffs themselves, the flatter vegetation of the clifftops (often derelict fields), and the soil beneath the vegetation.

Crossing the 4 miles (6.4km) of choppy sea between the little fishing port of Kilmore Quay in County Wexford and Great Saltee, I gradually become aware of large flocks of off-duty birds on the water around the colony. Getting closer to the islands there is persistent calling which eventually becomes a deafening clamour echoing off the rockfaces. Most of the noise comes from the kittiwakes, guillemots and razorbills, each of which seems to be constantly in dispute with its neighbours. The kittiwakes – small and noisy members of the gull family – cement their nests to near-vertical rockfaces with a mixture of green algae from the sea and their own droppings or guano. In the boulder clay which tops the rocky cliffs, small nesting depressions have been hollowed out by fulmars which sit incubating their single eggs. Although they look superficially like gulls in appearance, the fulmars are members of the petrel family and are easily distinguished in

Little Skeillig (Sceillig Bheag), County Kerry with the mist rolling off the sea. Almost every available space on this spectacular rock is covered with nesting gannets, over 22,000 pairs, making it one of the largest colonies in the world.

flight by their stiff-winged appearance. I have often stood on a windy clifftop and stared in amazement at the seemingly effortless flight of the fulmars soaring on an updraught of wind. Today these birds can be seen on all coasts of Ireland, but at the end of the last century the sight of a fulmar was a rare occurrence, mainly well out to sea off the west coast. Then, in 1911, the first pair was recorded breeding on the cliffs of north Mayo, and the expansion which followed was mirrored all around the eastern Atlantic. By the 1980s it was estimated that at least 30,000 pairs of fulmars nested in Ireland, and even today the cause of this remarkable population explosion is not clearly understood. Various explanations such as the increased food source in discarded fish offal from trawlers, the slight warming of the eastern Atlantic and even genetic changes in the birds themselves have been suggested.

Another seabird on the Great Saltee which has clearly benefited from the increase in commercial fishing activities is the gannet. Up to a hundred of these huge white birds with black wingtips have been seen diving and scrambling for discarded or escaped fish around trawlers during net-hauling and sorting of catches in the Irish Sea. Close to the fishing port of Howth, County Dublin, the latest Irish gannet colony has become established on Ireland's Eye as recently as 1989. But one of the most spectacular natural sights anywhere in Europe must be the gannet colony on the Little Skellig off County Kerry. If you take the boatride from the mainland at Portmagee, and undergo nearly an hour of battling into the Atlantic swell, you will finally reach the base of these rugged crags, which rise sheer out of the ocean. All around the boat gannets wheel over the waves and plunge-dive after fish in the crystal-clear waters. High up on the Little Skellig, every available space on the ledges is crowded with gannets and their fluffy white chicks. Even in calm weather, landing here is a dangerous task as the rocks are covered with a thick coating of slippery guano from generations of gannet droppings. In previous centuries this colony was plundered by boatloads of men with clubs who took large quantities of gannet chicks for salting. However, hunting ceased in the 1880s, and about twenty-five years later the colony had increased from a few dozen pairs to some 20,000 birds. By the 1980s there were over 22,000 gannet nest sites on this one rock and any further expansion here now seems impossible owing to lack of space.

Like the gannets, razorbills and guillemots on the neighbouring Great Skellig Rock are especially well adapted for life on these narrow ledges, often hundreds of yards above the sea. With their feet set well back near the tail, they sit upright, like penguins, facing the rock wall. With their back and wings they protect the single egg or chick from the wind and rain as well as from marauding neighbours. The eggs are pyriform (much more pointed than conventional eggs) so that if they are disturbed on a bare ledge they roll in a tight circle instead of going over the edge. The chicks remain still for most of the time to avoid getting knocked or blown off the ledge, but usually one of the parents is present to protect them until they can fend for themselves. The other adult is usually away at sea catching small fish such as sand eels or sprats which it disgorges on returning to the ledge. From a vantage-point on the clifftop, you can see that the colony below is a constant hive of activity. With whirring wings and much loud calling there are birds leaving and returning to the ledges throughout the daylight hours.

After dark, new sounds can be heard from the cliffs and sea around the colony. Putting your ear close to the crevices in a stone wall you can hear a strange 'churring' noise. This is the only evidence here of storm petrels, the smallest of the Irish sea birds. On the four outermost Blasket Islands, off County Kerry, storm petrels nest in tens of thousands among the scree slopes, from sea level to the summits of these precipitous islands. As the sun sinks below the horizon, large rafts of sea birds begin to form just offshore. Among the storm petrels are the other birds of the night, the Manx shearwaters and puffins. Under cover of darkness they make the dash to the land and flop to the ground before disappearing down a burrow entrance, for puffins, shearwaters and petrels are all easy prey on land to hungry great black-backed gulls. They leave their single chick alone underground for many hours before returning with a beakful of fish, hoping to avoid interception by the predatory gulls.

When I went to film the Manx shearwaters on the south west coast, I spent a spell-binding time on Inis Tuaisceart, an island which lies close to the Great Blasket. I had chosen a week when there would be no moon, as the birds will only arrive in large numbers if it is pitch dark. For the young shearwater chick lying in its burrow, this can mean spending many hungry hours waiting for a parent which might not land on the island for days! It is very difficult to describe the mystique and the atmosphere surrounding the Blasket Islands, especially during the nights of spring and summer. The build-up of sounds, from the quiet lapping of waves against the cliff face

The razorbill is distinguished by the rounded tip to its bill. The wings are short and pointed and the feet set well back, making the birds ideally adapted for 'flying' underwater in pursuit of shoals of fish. While one member of the pair is away fishing, the other incubates the egg or guards the single chick.

and the calls of various seabirds, to the increasing volume of the enchanting and eerie 'kuk-kuk-kuk-koo' calls of thousands of shearwaters arriving and piling into their burrows all over the island, is quite unbelievable. On these dark nights the masses of unseen birds passing overhead seem to come from nowhere. I often wonder what the reaction of a marooned sailor would be, left on that lonely island in the black of night and surrounded by the shearwaters' huge invisible orchestra of whirring wings and gurgling voices. Is it any wonder that the area is so rich in folk tales and in legends?

The neighbouring island of Inis Icíleáin is famous for a piece of music known as *Port na bPúcaí*, (*The Fairies' Lament*). Séamus Heaney refers to it in his poem 'The Given Note'. It is a very haunting piece of music which according to some is the sound of whales calling out to one another in the sea between the islands, or perhaps the sad singing chorus of grey seals, to which are added the calls of shearwaters. Others will tell you that it represents the voices of the island women keening for their loved ones, who have not returned from fishing trips in stormy oceans. But according to the islanders, *Port na bPúcaí* is a magic tune that was first heard being sung by a banshee *(beansí)* lamenting one of the island fairy folk who had died on Inis Icíleáin. There are words to the song, which several of the island people knew off by heart, but the tune was usually played on the fiddle. The international composer Seán Ó Riada, who took a great interest in the tune, remarked that *The Fairies' Lament* was not in any of the common modes and that it bore no relation whatsoever to any music familiar to the islanders at that time. Ó Riada first heard *Port na bPúcaí* being played by the Blasket Island fiddle player, Seán Cheaist Ó Catháin, and this inspired him to arrange the tune for the harpsichord.

On the Aran Islands off County Galway, razorbills, guillemots, black guillemots, puffins and cormorants were once a regular part of the islanders' diet. The flesh was also rendered down for oil for lamps which probably provided the only light in the houses. The landlord paid cash for the birds as their feathers were a valuable commodity at the market in Galway in the early nineteenth century and he would employ a skilled *ailleadóir* (cliffman) to do the catching. In his book *Stones of Aran*, Tim Robinson recounts how the cliffman would be lowered over the edge in the gathering dusk to crouch on a well-known ledge and await the arrival of the seabirds from their day at sea. In the pitch darkness he would crawl along the ledge, killing birds as he went with his bare hands and tying them them to a rope. By dawn, when he would be hauled up again bent with cold and cramp, the cliffman could have dispatched between 300 and 600 birds, according to contemporary accounts. In the early years of this century the islanders began to use nets to catch the birds, and the skills of the cliffmen became redundant.

In late summer, even before they have fully grown their flight feathers, young guillemots and razorbills glide down to their parents waiting on the sea, to begin their training for a life on the ocean waves. Their principal method of feeding is by plunge-diving from the surface to chase after shoals of small fish. Sometimes, in the midst of the chase, they may become entangled in a fishing net and drown, for all along the west coast of Ireland in summer there are mile upon mile of salmon drift nets, set in inshore waters to intercept the salmon returning from the ocean. They are made of

monofilament nylon and hang in the surface layers of the sea like an invisible curtain. The exact number of seabirds which perish in this way is impossible to measure because many are thrown overboard as the nets are hauled into the boats. Reports that thousands of auks had been killed in Galway Bay in 1976 led Dr Tony Whilde to carry out a survey in the following two years to try to establish the facts. He visited piers in the Galway Fishery district where salmon were landed and he estimated that the few hundred birds recovered or reported were only a small proportion of the total killed. The mortality was probably especially serious for the razorbill colony on the nearby Cliffs of Moher. Evidence from ringing recoveries shows that increasing numbers of razorbills and guillemots from Irish colonies such as Great Saltee are drowned in fishing nets, many off the coasts of Spain and Portugal in winter.

Walking along the top of the cliffs on Great Saltee I can feel a springy sensation under my feet as if I am treading on foam-filled cushions. These cushions are formed by typical maritime plants such as sea thrift, sea campion and scurvy grass, which are tolerant of salt spray and are covered in a mass of pink and white flowers in early summer. Clifftop vegetation can be heavily grazed by sheep or rabbits, which produces a maritime grassland with such species as red fescue grass and sea plantain. If the sward is kept short, it provides ideal feeding conditions for choughs. The distinctive call of the chough (*cág cos-dearg* or red-footed jackdaw) can be heard, winter and summer, from Great Saltee Island right around the west coast to Rathlin Island, County Antrim. The bright red legs and bill of this black crow give

Choughs are the red-legged crows of the west of Ireland. On the frost-free Atlantic coasts they can feed throughout the year by probing the soil for insects and catching sandhoppers on the strandline. Their nests are in caves or crevices on sea-cliffs and occasionally in disused mine shafts.

Top: The roseate tern is the rarest of the five tern species breeding in Ireland. It likes to nest in the shelter of dense vegetation such as lyme grass or tree mallow. The colony at Rockabill off the Dublin coast is the largest in Europe.

Middle: The arctic tern is an impressive long-distance migrant. Ireland is near the southern limit of its world breeding distribution. At least some birds winter in the sub-Antarctic and may therefore see more daylight than most other species.

Bottom: A common tern 'courtship feeding' its mate. These birds are quite aggressive in defence of the nest and will dive on and even strike any intruders to the colony. In mixed colonies other terns such as the rare roseate benefit from this 'protection'.

it a distinctive appearance when sighted feeding on a headland or beach. But to see a flock of these birds in flight over a stormy cliff is a delight never to be forgotten. They wheel and dive with the skill of fighter pilots, the primary flight feathers on their wingtips splayed wide apart. With the largest population in Western Europe, Ireland's choughs are of special conservation importance. They are primarily cliff-nesters using crevices and caves; occasionally, as on Valentia Island, County Kerry, they breed in disused mine shafts. I remember once visiting this old slate mine in June when the young choughs had just left the nest. The adult birds called loudly and insistently from outside as the novice fliers hopped about on the floor of the old mine searching for the entrance and freedom. The chough uses its long down-curved bill to probe the soil for insects and grubs, and flocks of these handsome birds can be seen in some places feeding on sandhoppers on the strandline. The chough's need for unfrozen soil and the mild, frost-free winters of the Atlantic seaboard may explain its maritime character compared with other members of the crow family. In winter choughs gather in large flocks and feed on the sand dunes where insect grubs can be found just below the dune vegetation. They prefer to feed in permanent grassland which has been grazed very short, so the high numbers of sheep grazing in western coastal areas today are helping to maintain the right feeding habitat. Choughs have declined around the northern coast of Ireland, apparently due to the fencing-off of the clifftop from grazing and consequent spread of scrub, but they are doing well elsewhere.

Grazing may not favour all clifftop species, however, although of those plants which are confined in Ireland to coastal cliffs and rocks only one is thought to be declining, being particularly sensitive to sheep-grazing. This is Scot's lovage, a dark green perennial, which has been recorded from five counties in the north-west of the country. It has not been recorded recently in the Republic of Ireland although it has been seen in a number of its Northern Ireland sites in Antrim and Derry. On exposed cliffs, such as the Cliffs of Moher, some very sensitive plants such as roseroot flourish in the absence of competition. Roseroot is not confined to the coast, being found also in inland rocky areas: its main European distribution is in the Arctic and the Alps. Other such species include Alpine meadow-rue, mountain avens, purple saxifrage, yellow mountain saxifrage, bearberry, holly fern and green spleenwort, all of which grow high on the cliffs at Slieve League, County Donegal.

One of the most remarkable clifftop plants is the tree mallow whose large purple flowers are more familiar from old cottage gardens by the seaside. On the tiny lighthouse island of Rockabill, off the County Dublin coast, it forms dense stands the height of a man. Most of the mallow now grows around the lighthouse buildings in the old gardens where, years ago, the lighthouse keepers grew vegetables to support themselves in the long months of winter isolation. Beneath the shelter of this veritable forest of tree mallow are hundreds of nesting roseate terns, forming the largest and most successful colony of the species in Europe. On one of my visits to the island to film the birds I was amazed by their tolerance of human presence, accustomed as they were to the constant company of the keepers. These hardy men had become their unofficial wardens, preventing unauthorized landings and removing the nests of any large gulls which threatened to occupy the breeding areas of the terns before they returned from Africa in the spring. Through the 1970s the European population of these handsome long-tailed sea birds had crashed to a fraction of its former numbers and some people blamed the hunting of the terns on West African coasts during the winter. But the crash also coincided with the natural erosion of some of the main Irish colonies at Tern Island in Wexford Harbour and Green Island in Carlingford Lough. About this time numbers began to increase at Rockabill, which soon became the Irish Sea headquarters of the species. The

lighthouse is now automatic and served by a helicopter as the last of the keepers left the island in 1989. Since then the island has been managed as an official refuge by the Wildlife Service and the Irish Wildbird Conservancy with full-time wardens in the summer months. The provision of wooden nest-boxes on the ground amongst the tree mallow has enabled the tern colony to produce even more young chicks in recent years, helping to replenish the Irish Sea population.

As I wander around a rocky headland on Great Saltee, County Wexford I see ample evidence of the erosive power of the sea – broken slabs, arches and

Dún Dúchathair (the black fort), Inis Mór, Aran Islands, County Galway. This pre-historic promontory fort is protected on two sides by sheer cliffs. Inside the walls are the remains of stone huts. The approach to the fort on the land side is protected by tall irregular standing stones known as chevaux-de-frise.

stacks, and dark, mysterious caves. Flat-bedded limestones such as those in Counties Sligo and Clare produce a stepped coastline with a wide, wave-cut platform at the high-tide mark. Older Palaeozoic rocks such as the Old Red Sandstones of County Kerry stand upright at the coast, giving a more rugged coastline. On the more exposed headlands such as Loop Head, County Clare, there are numerous storm beaches – great piles of boulders thrown up by the sheer power of mountainous seas, often over the top of the fields or roadways behind the shore. Littered with driftwood and other marine debris, these impressive beaches are too mobile for most plants and animals to survive except in a transitory state. On the less-exposed eastern coasts, such as those of Counties Wexford and Wicklow, there are also shingle beaches which have a distinctive flora. Seen from the air, one of the most impressive features is the 11 mile (18km) shingle beach called the Murrough which stretches from Greystones to Wicklow Town. In July, the large and showy yellow-horned poppy grows near the top of this beach among more common species like sea sandwort and sea rocket. The rare oyster plant, whose blue and pink flowers peep out from between the stones, was once widespread on the east coast but is now restricted to a few northern shingle beaches.

As I walk along the sand and shingle of the Murrough in spring, the first sign of birds nesting on the strandline may be the 'too-i, too-i' call of a solitary ringed plover. This familiar little wader with the distinctive pied pattern on its head and face and prominent black collar gives the distinct impression of a clockwork toy bird. It makes short runs of a few yards, stops to pick up some morsel and then tilts forward as if on a hinge. This is a feeding pattern common to its larger cousins, the golden plover, grey plover and lapwing. A simple scrape in the sand is all the ringed plover needs as a nest, and the four speckled eggs are perfectly camouflaged among the scattering of pebbles and shells along the beach. All plovers have a special method of protecting their young. Whenever I try following the ringed plover, it takes short bouts of flying around and then falls to the ground feigning injury. The closer I am to the chicks, hidden in a tussock of marram grass, the more excited the adult bird becomes.

Most Irish beaches have at most only a few pairs of ringed plover, but they are common and widespread. By contrast, the little tern is quite scarce and prefers to nest in small colonies. Its high-pitched call and jerky flight, as it hovers over the waves, are often the first signs that this elegant traveller has completed the long journey from its wintering grounds in Africa. It returns every spring to a few traditional mainland sites on the east coast, such as Baltray Dunes, County Louth, Kilcoole Beach, County Wicklow, and Raven Point, County Wexford. On the west coast there are little tern colonies on offshore islands such as the Aran Islands, County Galway, and the Inishkea Islands, County Mayo. Their main habitat requirements are a shingle beach which is relatively free from human disturbance and close proximity to shallow coastal water or a lagoon for fishing. When the terns breed successfully in a particular year, the colony can act as a honeypot for predators such as fox or kestrel. The little tern population in Ireland, although small and vulnerable, is relatively stable, and the birds move about between colonies from year to year according to local conditions.

Permanent animal residents on the surface of a sandy beach are few because of the constant blasting by the sand. But large pieces of driftwood provide at least a semi-permanent shelter for a few highly specialized creatures. I sometimes roll over large tree trunks on a sandy beach to see if I can find a black and yellow ground beetle, *Eurynebria complanata*, or a large woodlouse, *Armadillidium album*, scuttling for cover. These two characters are found only in the south-east of the country where there is sufficient summer sun on undisturbed beaches such as those of the Raven Nature Reserve near Wexford. In a storm the same piece of driftwood may act as a trap for sand blowing along the beach. So, too, do the plants, such as sea rocket and prickly saltwort, growing in the compost of seaweed along the driftline. As these pioneer plants grow through the spring and summer, a series of temporary embryo dunes form around them at the top of the beach. However, the storms of the following winter may reduce the level of the beach again by several yards.

Climbing the sand dunes at the back of the Raven beach, my legs are scraped by the blades of tough grasses, but little else grows among them except for the occasional prickly sea holly plant. True sand dunes are formed by the dune-building grasses – marram grass and the sand couch grass – which bind the mobile sand with their long underground rhizomes. In Ireland today there are few places where dunes are actively building as the sediments deposited on the sea floor after the last Ice Age have been exhausted and most wind-blown dune-building ceased in the Middle Ages. Where new foredunes do occur, such as at Magilligan, County Derry, or

The warning call of a nesting ringed plover is a common sound on sandy beaches in early summer. Using only a shallow scrape in the sand, it relies on camouflage to hide the eggs and will attempt to distract an intruder by feigning a broken wing.

Cottonweed is one of the rarest of Ireland's coastal plants. It is only found on one beach in south County Wexford where the movement of sand and shingle favour this attractive species. Some of the plants have been damaged by vehicle tracks on the beach.

Raven Point, County Wexford, they usually result from reworking of existing dunes around the estuary. Standing on top of the first dune ridge in a strong gale, it is easy to see how the marram grass traps the sand blown from the beach and fixes the dunes. In the nineteenth century there were numerous cases of drifting sands, usually caused by human activity. The marram grass was cut for thatching and bedding, and this disturbance, combined with the burrowing of rabbits which were encouraged for meat, often caused massive instability. Whole villages, such as Strandhill in County Sligo, were overwhelmed by drifting sand, and the inhabitants were forced to move to higher ground. In some places, such as Ballyness, County Donegal, or Inch, County Kerry, the dunes still appear to be highly mobile, with sand in constant circulation from beach to dunes to estuary and back to the beach again.

On the south coast of County Wexford, a number of coastal lagoons are linked together by barrier beaches which are quite different in character from other foredune areas in Ireland. Here, at Lady's Island Lake, the shingle barrier is topped by a thin crest of sand which is frequently overwashed by the sea on high tides backed by an onshore wind. Strong winds also move the sand over to the 'backshore' where it is deposited in the lagoon behind, and the whole barrier gradually moves inland. This unstable dune habitat is the only known location of one of Ireland's rarest coastal plants, the cotton weed. Its grey-green clumps can be seen here all year but the small golden flowers appear only in August. Cottonweed is widespread in western France and Portugal and it is at the northern limit

of its climatic range in Ireland.

Dropping down behind the first line of dunes there is welcome shelter from the wind and a sudden increase in diversity of plant and animal life. With a fixed sand surface, other plants can grow among the marram grass, with extensive cover of colourful flowers like bird's foot trefoil, lady's bedstraw, seaside pansy and mosses such as *Tortula ruraliformis*. In midsummer the flowers grow in a sheet of yellow which enlivens the otherwise monotonous green of the marram grass. In some places rare plants such as the bee orchid or the tall blue spikes of viper's bugloss grow in the fixed dune ridges. Common blue butterflies and the black and red burnet moths fly close to the food plants of their larvae. Few bird species nest on these open dunes because of the absence of trees and bushes. The skylark, however, is not hampered by the lack of songposts and maintains a steady hovering position in the sky while delivering its long and tuneful song. Meadow pipits are also plentiful on sand dunes and, in Ireland, these small, unimpressive birds act as the main hosts for the cuckoo.

Almost all Irish sand dunes are grazed by rabbits, preventing the development of woodland, although the presence of bluebells on some east coast dunes suggests that there were once woods here. Now an intermediate community, characterized by wild thyme, burnet rose and eyebright, is often present. Regular burning of the backdunes usually results in a vegetation dominated by bracken which can grow more than a yard (1m) high and makes walking here, from midsummer onwards, an uncomfortable experience.

As the calcium (seashell) element on the older dunes is leached out by

Plants which are specially adapted to withstand saltspray carried by the Atlantic winds, add a touch of colour to Ireland's sea-cliffs in spring and early summer.

centuries of rainfall, the surface layers of sand gradually become more acidic. Although common on British dune systems, the resulting dune heathland is rare in Ireland, possibly owing to heavy grazing pressure. However, at one sand dune nature reserve at Murlough, County Down, I have seen true dune heath dominated by ling and bell heather. Wherever gorse, blackthorn or hawthorn bushes grow on the backdunes there is usually an increase in birdlife, with linnet, wren and stonechat among the commonest species. An alien shrub, sea buckthorn, has been planted in some east and north coast dunes in an attempt to stabilize mobile sand, but it quickly becomes invasive and shades out the native flora. Its one redeeming feature is the heavy crop of orange berries which attract large flocks of migratory thrushes and finches in winter.

When walking through a natural dune system like that at Inch, County Kerry, I am often surprised to come upon wet areas with shallow pools and marshy vegetation around the edges. These are the slacks between dune

ridges where the sand surface has become deflated down to the permanent water table. Here creeping willow forms tangled mats of vegetation, with silverweed and sharp rush around the edges showing the height reached by the water table in winter. Orchids abound in these damp calcareous soils – broad-leaved marsh orchid and marsh helleborine are among the most common. Deeper water in the dune slacks allows the only toad in Ireland, the natterjack, to lay its characteristic strings of spawn in these pools. It is found in only a few coastal locations in County Kerry. I remember once finding one of these handsome amphibians, with the distinctive yellow stripe down its back, walking down a sandy path in front of me. Although it crawled quite slowly, never hopping like a frog, it was constantly on the move, a form of behaviour which makes it quite difficult to obtain a good photograph of the toad.

The dune slacks also provide a welcome source of drinking water for birds and mammals like badgers and foxes, which are both quite common in large

On the highly indented Connemara coastline patches of saltmarsh vegetation are draped between rocky points. Below the high tideline a thick growth of brown seaweed blankets the rocks providing numerous sheltered habitats for marine life.

sand dune systems. I remember a particular family of foxes living in the sand dunes at Tramore, County Waterford, which I observed being fed by a lady on horseback. Every morning at dawn, this equestrian animal-lover would arrive on the strand with her parcel of meat. The foxes always seemed to sense when their free meal was due and would lie in wait for the horse to appear. It was a most unusual ritual to observe - an elegant middle-aged lady astride a magnificent black mare, dropping pieces of meat after her in the sand and being followed through the dunes by a vixen and her string of five cubs!

One of the most extensive areas of dune slacks in Ireland once occurred in the dunes at Curracloe and Raven Point in County Wexford. However, much of this has been planted with coniferous trees and the northern part has been heavily modified for use as a caravan park. Only a small fringe of dunes at the southern tip remains in a relatively natural condition and this is now protected as a nature reserve. Another nature reserve at the North Bull

Island, only a few miles from the centre of Dublin city, is internationally important for wintering wildfowl as well as for the sand-dune system which holds two major golf courses, an interpretative centre and one of the most popular bathing beaches on the east coast. Protection of this nature reserve is largely a case of managing people. This includes limiting of areas to be used by vehicles, laying of path surfaces to prevent erosion, and helping visitors to appreciate the natural environment around them.

The damage caused by the development of golf links on sand dunes at Castlegregory, County Kerry, is now well established. The site is of national importance for conservation with a narrow dune system separating Lough Gill (itself an important wildfowl refuge) from the Atlantic Ocean. The development work involved lowering of some of the dunes using a mechanical digger; drainage of dune slacks and excavation of two ponds; resodding of areas along the lake shore to form greens; infilling along the lake shore extending the course into the lake; and rolling and mowing of

Atlantic waves at Ballyferriter, County Kerry. Exposed to the full might of the ocean, the west coast of Ireland has some of the roughest seas in western Europe. But they are also some of the clearest waters and ideal for scuba diving.

Machair at Aillebrack, County Galway. This habitat is unique to the Atlantic fringes of Ireland and Scotland where the shelly sands have been blasted into a flat plain by high winds. The grasslands are rich in plant species and of special importance to nesting waders such as lapwing, ringed plover and dunlin.

dune vegetation. The marram grass zone in the foredunes has been reduced to less than half its former width, exposing the sand underneath to wind erosion. Lowering of the water table in the dune slacks has caused a marked reduction in diversity in the vegetation and the loss of a number of plant species including marsh orchids. Mowing and fertilizer application in the consolidated dunes has also reduced plant diversity by almost a half, again leading to the loss of some species including pyramidal orchids and the rare lady's tresses. On the lake shore the formerly herb-rich meadow has been converted to a monotonous short turf dominated by red fescue, and the fringing reeds have been removed along with a significant proportion of a rare plant unknown elsewhere in County Kerry. An important breeding and foraging area for the rare natterjack toad has been destroyed at the core of its limited range in Ireland. The basic problem is that golf courses are exempt from the normal requirement for planning permission and, with the growth in popularity of golf, development pressures will inevitably continue.

The north-west coasts, from the Inishowen Peninsula in County Donegal to Galway Bay, have a unique kind of sandy plain or machair (from the Irish word *machaire*). This is best developed in the north-west corner of County Mayo around the Mullet Peninsula, which is one of the windiest places in Europe. By early June the machair plain is a mass of colourful flowers, with the familiar seaside pansy and the moss *Tortula ruraliformis* in drier parts and glaucous sedge and bird's foot trefoil in the damper areas. The sand is highly calcareous because of the high proportion of shell fragments blown inland from the beach. The vegetation, closely grazed by cattle and sheep, provides ideal nesting conditions for lapwing. As I walk in from the beach, the adult birds rise from the ground and circle in the air above me with plaintive cries warning any young chicks on the ground to freeze. Dry, wind-eroded machair plains often grade into damp marshy grassland on the edge of small coastal loughs. Some beautiful and delicate flowers, such as the white grass-of-parnassus and deep purple marsh orchids, grow here. The best examples of wet machair grassland are found at places such as Termoncarragh Lake and Doaghtry Lough in County Mayo. Here there are many small winding channels and pools, a habitat which closely resembles the wetter parts of blanket bogs. The trilling calls of dunlin reveal the presence of these enigmatic waders here in May and June. Unlike the lapwings they are secretive birds and often prefer to leave the nest by walking quietly away from an intruder.

The machair is a habitat which has resulted from the interaction of man and nature over many thousands of years. Archaeological finds in the extensive machair plains around Doonloughan, near Slyne Head, County Galway, show that in the Bronze Age this area held a thriving community with well-developed farming systems. Heavy grazing pressure in recent centuries has reduced the sward to a dense and species-rich community but, in places, has also broken the thin skin of vegetation, allowing fierce Atlantic gales to rip gullies through the soft sand below. Unlike the sand plains of the Scottish Outer Hebrides, few machair plains in western Ireland are cultivated, but many are used intensively for recreation. Sports pitches, caravan parks and, more recently, golf courses are widespread, and the pressure of disturbance increases with the growing amount of human leisure time. The flat dry surface of the machair plain makes it ideal for use as an airstrip, and swathes of mown grass and tarmacadam can be found in such remote and beautiful places as Inishmore in the Aran Islands and Carnboy in west Donegal.

At one time the machair plains of the Mullet stretched virtually unbroken as far as the eye could see down the western fringe of this wild peninsula. They were owned in common by the people of the nearby villages and townlands but the government's Land Commission encouraged the practice of subdivision or 'striping' of the coastal land. A walk on the machair today invariably means climbing over post and wire fences and the remote and wild atmosphere has been destroyed. Yet there is a ray of hope with the possibility of support from the new EC Common Agricultural Policy for traditional, low-intensity farming practices in these areas. The designation of one area of machair at Slyne Head, County Galway, as an Environmentally Sensitive Area (ESA) is a small but promising step in the right direction.

3

RIVER
AND WETLAND

*A spate river rises rapidly and the Cladys is no exception. The lough
from which it flows is a basin among the mountains, the sides of
which are scored with rivulets. Errigal is the chief of these, the highest
in Donegal. It first put on its 'nightcap', a sort of cloud halo,
which rapidly began to spread down its sides, and ultimately enveloped it,
wiping out every trace of its towering wall, 2,500ft. (769m) high.
Then the lough itself seemed to be one with the rain, and was
churned white. The river soon leaps into life under such conditions,
and what a metamorphosis next day! Its rocky beds became
seething rapids, its rivulets changed into swift currents,
the tinkling falls took on a diapason roar. A single stream grew
into a dozen, which scampered and jostled one another
like pent-up children let loose from school.*

Joseph Adams,
The Angler's Guide to the Irish Fisheries, 1923

*A waterfall plunges into the glacial valley of
Glenmacnass, County Wicklow. The typical
U-shape of the valley was sculptured by ice
over 10,000 years ago and the modern river
meanders across the fertile valley floor.*

A weir on the River Dargle, which was washed away by heavy floods during the late 1960s. This magical place reflected every mood of the river from quiet waters to roaring torrents.

The County Brook which divides Dublin from Wicklow flowed past our bedroom window, and the River Dargle, which was on the other side of the house, ran only a few yards beyond the kitchen. Growing up in the Dargle Valley meant that I had always had the sound of a waterfall in my ears, a lullaby without which I could hardly sleep. Most of the music came from the weir, a most magical place for wildlife. Above the weir, the river was flat and slow-moving. It seemed to hesitate before crossing this solid concrete barrier and then rushed down the moss-covered slope into two large fish-pools below. Waterhens (moorhens), wild duck and kingfishers nested along the flats above the tumbling cascade. A patient heron stood forever motionless at the edge. He was part of the landscape. He waited and waited at this spot, where some unsuspecting eel or trout with an urge to find new ground further upstream would make the supreme effort of trying to swim up the fall. Quick as lightning, the grey statue would come to life and, with a rapid stab of its rapier-like beak, the victim was grabbed from the water and swallowed head first.

This part of the Dargle, where we lived, was a meeting place for a great variety of birds, insects, fish and mammals. The tumbling water suited many small aquatic animals, it had food for both fish and birds, and for mammals it provided a crossing place. There were eels, trout, sticklebacks, minnows, stone loach and lampreys. The harmless loach was known to the local boys as a 'stinger', because of its set of whiskers. They never referred to the lamprey as anything but a bloodsucker, because of its habit of attaching itself to a stone by holding on with its peculiarly shaped mouth. The young

mottled brown herring gulls were called horse gulls, and siskins were known only as devines. My favourite river birds were the kingfisher, because of its exquisite colouring, and the dipper, which amazed us all by regularly walking underwater in its hunt for caddis larvae. There were wildlife programmes to be seen through our window every day. These sightings of animals were my first contact with what were to be many future friends.

Few pictures of Ireland would be complete without some freshwater. The famous lakes of Killarney feature in almost every tourist brochure, and the River Shannon flows gently past the monastic ruins of Clonmacnoise in the midlands. Irish culture is full of watery images such as the beautiful traditional song 'Cois Abainn Na Séad' ('By the River of Gems'), Séan Ó Riada's composition 'On the Banks of the Sullane', and W. B. Yeats's poem 'The Lake Isle of Innisfree', to mention but three. While we value the images and beauty of Irish waters, we have a tendency to forget the tangible benefits which freshwater provides. Drinking water, inland fisheries, wildlife habitats, power generation and dilution of waste are some of the more obvious ones. For a small island off the western fringe of Europe, Ireland's freshwater resources are impressive. Lough Neagh has the largest surface area of any freshwater body in Ireland or Britain. The Shannon is the longest river in these islands. Irish turloughs (seasonal lakes) are unique in Western Europe. Water is so much a part of our lives that we take it all for granted.

Lying in the path of the moisture-filled winds from the Atlantic, Ireland has an almost constant rainy season. The number of rain-days per year ranges from an average of 190 near the east and south-east coasts to about

The Caher river is one of the few surface waters in the Burren region, County Clare where most of the rivers run underground. The lime-rich waters support abundant insect life and some small brown trout feed in the river.

The dipper is superbly adapted for life in fast-flowing streams and rivers where it feeds on the insect life beneath the surface. The distinctive white bib is easy to spot as it bobs about among the boulders and tumbling water.

250 days in places near the west coast. After small losses due to evaporation and transpiration by plants, the average effective rainfall on the land is still relatively high, and about two-thirds of this drains away to the sea as surface run-off in rivers and lakes. The remainder filters into the earth and moves slowly through the soil and rock to emerge again in rivers or the sea. Because most of Ireland's mountains are around the rim of the island there are many fast-flowing short rivers; those which emerge from the relatively flat central plain, such as the Shannon and the Boyne, are quite slow-flowing in their middle courses. The long River Bann, which flows across the north-east corner of Ireland, is subdivided by Lough Neagh. The natural productivity of freshwaters and hence of their wildlife communities is directly related to the underlying geology, with the greatest contrast between the lime-rich waters of the midlands and west and the acidic waters of the mountain ranges around the coastal fringe.

The simplest freshwater systems in Ireland are the mountain lakes which nestle in corries and deep valleys carved out by the glaciers of the last Ice Age. The brown peat-stained water drains directly from the mountain blanket bogs covering the high slopes which are formed of acidic rock types such as granite, schist and quartzite. One of the most conspicuous features of these acid lakes is the lack of marginal vegetation; shorelines mostly consist of bare sand or stones. This is due to the low levels of dissolved nitrogenous and phosphorus compounds which are essential plant foods. A few submerged plants such as quillwort grow here but they are rarely visible on the surface. Brown trout live in these lakes but they do not grow large because of the poor feeding conditions. Related to them is the arctic char which was once widespread but now occurs only in a few deep mountain lakes. This unique race of fish is here at the southern edge of its world range and is thought to have survived as an isolated population at the leading edge of the last glaciation.

Whenever I go walking along the banks of a swift-flowing mountain stream I am constantly on the lookout for a small brown bird, bobbing up and down on a boulder in midstream with a strange, almost clockwork twitch. This is the dipper, looking like a large, plump version of a wren, its white apron glinting in the sunlight. If I get too close, it takes off and flies low over the water down the middle of the stream until, at a safe distance from me, it lands on a familiar perch. I watch carefully to see the dipper 'plop' into the water and disappear. It can stay underwater for up to half a minute and seems undaunted by even the fastest currents which would sweep away any other songbird and drown it. The dipper is unique among birds in its ability to walk along the bottom of the stream, turning over small stones as it goes and picking off larvae of insects such as caddis flies and mayflies. The white apron-like pattern on its breast seems to act as a reflector while it searches for food and has earned the bird its Irish name, *gabha dubh* (blacksmith). The dipper's dependence on these freshwater invertebrates makes it a good indicator of water quality because in polluted streams there may be insufficient food for the birds. Dippers are also known to be sensitive to an increase in acidity of freshwater which can result from rainfall containing dissolved sulphur dioxide.

Whilst acid rain is a major problem for freshwaters in the rest of Europe, it is almost unknown in Ireland. The majority of Ireland's lakes are in limestone areas where the high dissolved carbonate levels are sufficient to neutralize any artificial acidity. The freshwater systems most sensitive to acidification are those whose catchments include a lot of granite or quartzite with thin soils which are poorly buffered against acidification. As most of Ireland's rain comes from clouds moving in from the Atlantic Ocean, we are fortunate to be up-wind of the worst of Europe's polluting industry. But

The discharge of concentrated organic matter such as silage effluent into a river produces a rapid growth of algae which uses up all the oxygen, killing fish and aquatic insects.

occasionally acid rain has been recorded on the east coast of Ireland in short periods of easterly winds, especially in late spring and early summer. The effects of this increased acidity on the ecosystems have been studied in two mountain lakes on opposite sides of the country. Detailed studies of the plankton, macroinvertebrates, fish stocks and aquatic flora show a much lower diversity of all groups in the eastern lake and complete absence of some animals such as mayflies, molluscs and crustaceans which are very sensitive to increased acidity. The brown trout in the eastern lake at Glendalough, County Wicklow, are much slower-growing than their counterparts in the west at Lough Maumwee, County Galway, and eel and salmon fry are completely absent in the former. It is known that with increased acidity such elements as aluminium become more soluble and are released from the soil. Quite low concentrations of aluminium dissolved in the water can be lethal to certain freshwater organisms, and non-lethal effects such as impaired growth and reproduction can cause eventual decline and disappearance of some animals. Hence the absence of dippers on an otherwise suitable upland stream suggests that chemical changes in the waters may have affected their food supply.

Irish dippers have long been regarded as a race separate from those in Britain and the rest of Europe, but apart from a slightly darker plumage there seem to be few other distinctions. Certainly their size and weight and the growth rate of the nestlings of Irish dippers are remarkably similar to those of other races. Nest-building begins early in February or March, allowing time for some pairs to raise a second family during the long summer days. The nest itself is a large, untidy dome of moss, grass and leaves, sometimes as big as a football, with a single small hole for an entrance. The same traditional nest sites are used year after year, the majority being located under bridges. The cavities in old crumbling stonework suit the dipper well, but modern steel girders are equally acceptable if they provide enough of a ledge above the water. Sometimes the nest is built among tree roots on the river bank or even behind a waterfall, but man-made locations seem to be preferred. One pair on the River Moygannon, County Down, even chose to make their home in the boot of an upturned car which some thoughtful human had added to the scenery of the river.

As all the tributary streams merge to form a main river channel, subtle changes occur in the freshwater ecology. As the channel becomes wider, the water moves at a more leisurely pace. A mixture of silt and sand, which has been carried along in suspension, begins to settle out on the river bed, and plants can take root. Then the river enters a sequence of pools, glides (smooth-flowing sections) and riffles (shallows). The level of plant nutrients begins to change as the river moves into its lowland phase and acidity of the water is reduced. The growth of long trailing plants such as water crowfoot provides convenient settling places for freshwater snails and the larvae of caddis flies and mayflies. The abundance of food and shelter among the river plants in the glides attracts large numbers of brown trout, the most widely distributed of our freshwater fishes. These are the resident trout of the rivers and lakes and, owing to their long isolation in particular freshwater systems, several different, genetically distinct, races of brown

Young sea trout. In recent years populations of these fish have been decimated as they move from rivers to shallow coastal waters. Here they are attacked by parasitic sea lice which are thought to originate from the coastal salmon farms in these areas.

trout have evolved in Ireland. In his *Studies on Loch Melvin*, Andy Ferguson of Queen's University, Belfast, states: 'There are good grounds for treating gillaroos, sonaghan and ferox as distinct and separate species of trout.' The variety of habitat conditions on the river bed is important to the fish in each stage of its lifecycle. From late October the adult trout lay their eggs in the gravel bed of the river, and when they hatch in spring the juveniles move to the pool areas of the stream.

The sea trout, which many Irish anglers know as the white trout *(breac geal* – bright trout), is common around the Irish coast. It is a migratory form of the brown trout but its behaviour is quite distinct. In his book *The Angler in Ireland*, 1989, Dr Ken Whelan of the Salmon Research Agency at Burrishoole, County Mayo states:

> In all sea trout populations studied to date, females dominate. The ratio of females to males may vary from 60:40 per cent to 80:20 per cent, but in all cases it is the egg-laying female which is most likely to migrate to the sea. It is tempting to speculate on the survival value to the species of this adaptation but in reality we have little real basis for such conjecture. It is obvious, however, that the resident male brown trout play a far greater role in the maintenance of our sea trout stocks than previously imagined.

I remember when fishermen used to regard every small brown trout caught in a sea trout fishery as a nuisance, but these recent studies have changed people's attitudes and shown the importance of protecting our juvenile stocks of brown trout.

During the clear days of winter, one of the thrills of wildlife-watching is to discover salmon spawning in a clear stretch of water where they can be clearly seen at close quarters. December is the month when salmon choose to spawn, and my observations of these activities have been mostly during Christmas week. It is probably a wise choice for the fish as they are less

Above: Ned Maguire, who was one of Ireland's best-loved anglers, fly-fishing on the Kings River, County Kilkenny. Fishermen are the self-appointed guardians of Irish rivers and lakes and they are usually the first to take action whenever problems arise which threaten these important habitats.

Right: Giant hogweed (Heracleum mantegazzianum) on the banks of the River Dargle, County Wicklow. This introduced species which originally came from south-west Asia, is up to 8ft (5m) tall and has a stem of up to 3 inches (10cm) thick. Each year, it produces a mass of seed which falls into the river and is transported to other parts of the valley. The sap produced by the stems of this plant can cause painful skin lesions if touched, especially in sunny weather.

obvious during these short days of low light when rivers are at their winter level. The urge to breed is so strong that I have seen salmon in Connemara running out of a lake and up into a shallow stream barely 2ft (60cm) wide. These small waterways offer little or no protection to adult fish so the salmon would run straight back to the lake as soon as they had finished spawning.

The salmon has been swimming in Irish waters since long before the first people arrived, and no other fish receives as much mention in Irish folklore. Its image has always been linked to health and strength, and a customary saying when raising one's glass is *'sláinte an bhradáin agus croí folláin'* ('the health of the salmon and a sound heart'). The best-known story about this king of fish concerns the legendary Gaelic hero Fionn mac Cumhaill, who ate the Salmon of Knowledge. It is said that forever after that nothing was unknown to Fionn.

As I grew up on the banks of the River Dargle, the really exciting days were the flood times. It took two days of heavy rain to turn the Dargle from a small, clear and fairly easy-flowing river into a mud-coloured roaring torrent. As the water level rose rapidly, it had the effect of making the weir sink from view. The salmon pools then disappeared and the Dargle raced completely out of control in a mad rush seawards. For us, it was a good lesson in the power of water. At its normal level the Dargle was by no means a large river. However, its small size was never an indication of its importance as a nursery for salmon and sea trout. From April to May the whole river seemed to teem with silvery smolt of about 4-6inches (10-15cm)

in length. These were the fish which had changed their trout-like river outfits for sea suits of sparkling silver. They were baby sea trout and salmon answering the call of the Atlantic and working their way downstream towards the estuary. These smolt would probably spend several years in the sea, with the young salmon travelling even as far as Greenland in search of rich feeding while the sea trout would just move around the Irish coast. Eventually the urge to return would drive the fish back in the direction of home, and instinct would then steer them to their spawning beds in their native river.

These were the magnificent fish that we would see from our window, jumping, leaping and tumbling as they battled with their first obstacle since exchanging their saltwater habitat for a freshwater one. For fresh-run salmon and sea trout, the weir was only a temporary barrier. They were as full of energy as the wild Atlantic which had fed them for the past few years. If the rush of water over the fall was too strong, they would try again and again, sometimes moving to another part of the weir to make another mighty leap into the swirling flood waters. It was a wonderful spectacle. The first migrants to arrive were the large sea trout of 3-4lb (1.3-1.7kg), which were the spring fish. They would usually swim into the first flood in June. In the following weeks would come the large runs of salmon weighing from 6-24lb (2.7-9kg) and along with them would travel in their hundreds the shoals of sea trout weighing anything from 8oz to 3lb (225g to 1.3kg). These smaller sea trout, which were returning to the Dargle for the first time, were always known in this part of County Wicklow as 'clowns'. According to my father, the name must have been in existence for a long time, as 'clown' was really the Irish *caille abhainn* (river maiden), which is just what these fresh-run sea trout were!

The speed of the current has a great effect on the invertebrate life which can survive in lowland rivers. The river bends with the shape of the landscape, and gravel is deposited on the bank where the current is fast, silt

The freshwater pearl mussel is protected by law from pearl-hunting but it is very sensitive to pollution and has declined throughout its range.

and mud where it slows. Freshwater pearl mussels live in fast-flowing rivers which are normally low in calcium. They are found mainly in sandy gravel close to the river banks and they are very sensitive to enrichment of the water by organic pollution. Individual mussels can live for more than fifty years and they reproduce very slowly compared with other molluscs. Only rarely do these large bivalves contain pearls, but over-exploitation by amateur pearl-hunters and water pollution has brought this remarkable species close to extinction in Europe. Now Ireland is one of the few strongholds for the freshwater pearl mussel and it is specially protected by law here. A unique local form of the mussel known as *durrovensis* survives in a short stretch of the River Nore in County Laois. It is thought that this form became isolated here after the last Ice Age.

Despite the abundance of freshwater habitats in Ireland today, the meltwater lakes which covered the Irish landscape after the Ice Age must have been quite inhospitable places. Of the three species of amphibian in Ireland, only one, the common newt, is thought to have recolonized the island in this period, before it was cut off from the rest of Europe by rising sea levels. Often mistaken for lizards because of their reptile-like features, newts hibernate over winter on land, under stones or in the soil. They wake in early spring and migrate to the edges of ponds and lakes when the male develops a prominent crest along the length of his back and tail. Compared with the dull-coloured female, the male newt in breeding condition takes on a range of bright greens and browns with darker speckles and stripes along his sides. He even has the ability, like certain fish, to change body colour to provide camouflage against a particular habitat background. The eggs are laid one at a time, usually attached to vegetation in shallow water.

Few people have ever observed a pair of newts reproducing, but it is difficult to ignore the spawning of frogs. I remember walking by a very slow-moving stream in February and being quite puzzled by a continuous faint noise, not unlike the distant sound of a chain-saw. Then a sudden movement in the water caught my attention and it quickly became clear that the surface was a mass of frogspawn and writhing, fat-bodied frogs. The noise was coming from the males as they jostled for position to mount the females and fertilize the thousands of eggs being produced. The eggs quickly swell when they absorb water, and the masses of spawn can fill the stream from bank to bank. At spawning the frogs are usually quite sluggish and provide easy prey for a number of larger creatures, especially herons which are themselves building up their body condition for nesting and egg-laying at this time of year.

Ireland's wet climate is ideal for the heron (or crane as it is commonly known here), which is found almost everywhere there is surface water, both inland and on the coast. When it catches a frog or small fish, the heron will swallow it whole, with a visible lump passing down the long neck. Larger fish such as eels take a bit longer to deal with, and I have seen a heron wrestling with a large eel which had wrapped its tail several times around the bird's neck. The nineteenth-century Irish naturalist William Thompson told in his book *Natural History of Ireland* (1850) of a heron picked up almost dead on the shores of Belfast Lough. Stuck in its throat was an eel 26 inches (65cm) long and 4½ inches (11.25cm) in diameter. No wonder the poor

A grey heron stalks the shallow waters in search of fish or frogs. At other times it will stand motionless waiting for potential prey to swim within reach of the long sword-like bill.

bird felt ill! Irish rivers and lakes are full of eels, but the heron's very varied diet also includes flatfish, water birds, beetles and even small rodents. Feeding territories along the river bank or estuary are vigorously defended against other herons, and birds have even been known to kill each other. The best feeding is often in the half-light of dawn or dusk when the still form of a hunting heron blends into the shadows. Its large wings and slow, laborious flight make the bird an easy target and some are still shot at fish farms and on valuable salmon fisheries. In the last century herons were occasionally eaten, and William Thompson recalled one such dinner in County Donegal: 'A young heron was served up roasted at the table and proved excellent, the flavour resembling that of hare, as did the dark colour of the flesh.' He added that the birds were sometimes buried in the earth for several days to remove the fishy taste.

Most of the centre of Ireland is a flat plain across which the River Shannon flows from north to south. The Shannon is not only one of the longest rivers in Europe but also one of the most unspoilt. When asked for his views on this great waterway, the eminent Irish scientist Professor Frank Mitchell replied: 'The Shannon is a very strange river. It has no valleys so it just meanders along through the countryside.' In its central section between the great lakes of Lough Ree and Lough Derg it falls only 39ft (12m) in height over a distance of 29 miles (48km), which gives it a shallower gradient than any other large river in Europe. And unlike most major European rivers, whose lower reaches have by now been contained within flood barriers, the Shannon overflows its banks every winter and spreads out to form a slow-moving shallow wetland. These seasonally flooded grasslands are known in Ireland as callows and are of international importance for their wildlife in both summer and winter.

Towards the end of April every year the winter floods begin to recede and the callows emerge into the sunshine. I have sometimes been in the area at dawn on a misty spring morning and seen small parties of whimbrels as they move northwards, using the river as a corridor in their return migration to Icelandic breeding grounds. Their liquid, whistling calls echo across the water and mingle with the mewing cries of the first lapwings circling over their own nest sites on the water's edge. Already the first of the typical callow plants, the marsh marigold, is providing a bright touch of spring with its large yellow flowers. The soils, still saturated by the winter floods, provide ideal feeding conditions for waders like the whimbrels, which probe with their long bills, and lapwings, which pick up insects among the emerging vegetation. In an average year cattle are not put out to graze on the callows until May at the earliest because of the soft ground and the slow growth of grass. Heavy rains during the early part of the spring can be a definite advantage to the birds and plants as grass-cutting is then delayed until the land is sufficiently dry for mowing machines to operate. This provides the all-important time and space for ground-nesting birds to complete their breeding cycle, at least to the stage where the chicks are able to follow their parents to the cover of taller vegetation.

The long damp fields of the Shannon callows are divided in place of fences by deep drains, themselves filled with plants such as the yellow water lily and yellow iris. In the uncut meadows among the sedges and meadowsweet, rare plants such as the delicate marsh pea are able to flower and set seed before the mower takes its toll. At Clonmacnoise, County Offaly, the marsh pea has actually increased its area of growth in fields which are lightly fertilized. In most years a good crop of late hay is cut from these meadows, but occasionally summer rains damage the crop. In this respect, little has changed here since the nineteenth century when the Report of the Shannon Commissioners for 1838 recorded: 'The summer and autumn being wet, the hay was injured both by rain and floods, and in some places nearly destroyed.' In October, with predictable regularity, the river overflows its banks and spreads out across the fields, forming a long, shallow lake. This coincides with the arrival of great flocks of wild duck, geese and swans from their Arctic breeding grounds in Greenland, Iceland and Siberia. They congregate in mixed flocks, their haunting calls echoing across the swelling river. I imagine that, to the eye of a whooper swan, the swirling silver waters of the Shannon must look quite similar to the treeless, watery landscape of the tundra which it left behind in Iceland just a few short weeks before. Except for the occasional wildfowler, few people venture out on the callows in winter, and the wildlife is relatively undisturbed. For this reason, shy animals like the otter often come out in daylight on the banks of the river.

The footprints of an otter are quite obvious when seen in soft mud on a river bank. The webbing between the five toes shows up clearly, and the long heavy tail often trails along making a mark like the keel of a boat. If there is an obstruction such as a weir across the river, an otter will often

The marsh orchid appears in June among the bracken and yellow rattle of a hay meadow on the banks of the River Shannon. Winter flooding, undisturbed soils and the absence of artificial fertilizer are the main factors which produce a rich flora in these grasslands.

leave the water at this point, and its regular passing makes a well-used trail through the vegetation. Man-made structures like weirs and bridges are also used by the otters as convenient places to leave behind their distinctive droppings or spraints. When fresh these are quite black and slimy-looking and often contain large quantities of fish bones and scales making them spiky in appearance. When I find a spraint, I usually get down on my knees for a quick sniff because, once I smell the musty, fishy odour, I can be sure it was left by an otter. As well as being a means of discarding the inedible hard parts of their prey, spraints are used for communication between the otters which often travel alone. Each dropping is like a 'smellogram' which probably defines the age and sexual status of the caller and can be read only by another otter. To make sure that other otters will find the spraints, they are usually left in quite prominent positions on ledges beneath bridges, on boulders in midstream or on the top of grassy tufts known as 'seats'. They are often found near the meeting of two streams or where a river enters a lake, as if these places are well-used crossroads in the otter's world.

The otter is probably more common and widespread in Ireland than in any other country in north-west Europe. It occurs on most rivers, canals, lakes, lowland bogs and on the south and west coasts where it is found widely on rocky shores and offshore islands. Little was known about the true distribution of the otter in Ireland until 1981, when a systematic survey was carried out throughout the entire country by Peter and Linda Chapman of the Vincent Wildlife Trust. Using a technique based on the presence or absence of otter spraints or other signs, they were able to show that otters, occurred at 92 per cent of surveyed sites. No large areas of the country were devoid of otters and all sites visited on the west coast had positive signs. Comparable surveys in Britain found otter signs at 73 per cent of sites in Scotland, 20 per cent in Wales and only 6 per cent in England. In Ireland they are known to frequent river banks in some of the major towns and spraints have even been found at O'Connell Bridge in the heart of Dublin.

Otters are often accused of damaging stocks of salmon and trout, but analysis of both stomach contents and spraints shows that they have a very wide-ranging diet and will take whatever is most readily available in particular waters. Eels feature strongly on the menu both in freshwater and on the coast and, as eels prey on salmon eggs, this could be seen as a benefit to fisheries. Salmon spawn in freshwater in midwinter, and the spent fish, exhausted after the effort of reproduction, are easy prey to an otter. Other fish such as perch, rudd and sticklebacks are often taken, whilst waterhens and their flightless chicks make an easy meal in the breeding season. When frogs are spawning in traditional ponds and streams in early spring, otters may gorge themselves on these amphibians which are too absorbed in the process of reproduction to jump or swim away. Although the otter usually takes the food most easily available to it, in a situation where there is a large concentration of fish, even though these may be outside its everyday diet, an otter could see it as an opportunity to catch a meal fairly effortlessly. This sometimes happens where shoals of salmon and sea trout gather in an estuary or at the foot of a fall in preparation for their journey upstream to the spawning beds.

The limestone central plain and the poorly draining soils of the west and north-west are dotted with lakes which, in total, constitute about 2 per cent of the land surface of Ireland. One of the most attractive insects of these waterways is the mayfly or greendrake *(Ephemera danica)*. I find it a very enjoyable experience to sit by a limestone lake on a calm day in late May and watch the swarms of these insects after they have emerged from their nymphal skins, sitting on the water while their delicate legs prevent the body from coming into contact with the surface. Some become airborne almost immediately; while others rest awhile before flying off to rest in the nearest trees. The colder the weather, the longer they seem to remain sitting on the water. These very large flies live for about two years as nymphs on the bottom of the lake, where they excavate a burrow in the mud with their specially adapted mandibles. The mayfly's jaws are fashioned to feed on vegetable matter, including algae, and its only defence at this stage is its ability to hide. The insect's life-span on dry land, however, is very short, a few days at most. It is quite a sight to watch the mayfly's nuptial flight, which usually takes place in the afternoon. Large clouds of the insects gather together in the air and begin their hovering flight, rising and falling continuously and taking up a position in the lee of bushes or trees if conditions become windy. After mating, the females fly out to deposit their eggs on the surface of the lake or river, and on completing that activity they fall on to the water to die. This is the time of year when heavy trout, deeming it worth their while to rise to this wonderful feast of insects, can often be captured quite easily on rod and line. It is for this reason that the mayfly season has become known to anglers as the Duffers' Fortnight!

Declining fish stocks in some lakes have sometimes been blamed by anglers on the otter's smaller North American cousin, the feral mink. Best-known for their pelt, these animals were first introduced to Ireland on fur farms in the 1950s. Most of these early enterprises were small and unregulated, and there were many escapes of mink into the wild. Selective breeding in captivity produces a range of colours, including silvery grey, but feral mink breeding in the wild quickly revert to their natural coat colour, usually dark brown or black. I remember once watching a solitary mink swimming across a midland lake, quite unconcerned by my presence. Less agile in the water than an otter, it was swimming directly towards a patch of reeds, its thick bushy tail floating on the surface behind it. Through my binoculars I could see what it was after as it climbed on to the floating nest of a coot. If there were eggs there it would have sucked them all and any chicks which had hatched would not have lasted long. Water-birds such as coots, moorhens and duck form a regular part of the feral mink's diet: for example, they are known to prey on nesting ducks such as the common scoter, which breeds on the northern fringe of Europe, in Iceland and Scandinavia, with a small population in Scotland and Ireland. On Lower Lough Erne in County Fermanagh the numbers of breeding scoter grew steadily during the first half of this century, reaching about 150 pairs in 1967. These small black ducks breed under dense scrub on the numerous islands in the lake where they are free from most ground predators such as foxes. However, since the early 1970s few young ducklings were successfully reared, and from 1978 onwards the total number of scoters here dropped dramatically. This posed a real puzzle as there was no evidence of a general population decline in Ireland, with the scoters on Lough Conn, County Mayo, remaining relatively stable over the same period. The most obvious change in Lough Erne was a marked decline in water quality coinciding with increased sewage, fertilizer and industrial inputs throughout the Erne catchment. The water here had become distinctly cloudy compared with the crystal clear waters of Lough Conn, and this had direct implications for the scoters which feed on bottom-dwelling invertebrates such as water snails, mayfly nymphs and midge larvae. Sampling of the beds of both lakes showed that the numbers of these creatures were much lower on Lough Erne but that there were high numbers of the freshwater louse *Asellus,* confirming the polluted conditions there. The picture emerged that the hatching success of scoters was comparable on the two lakes but that few ducklings survived on Lough Erne where they were simply starving to death. Feral mink were present on Lough Erne before the decline in scoters began but this has not protected them from blame: the matter remains unresolved.

A mink will prey on almost anything of suitable size which it finds near the water's edge. Slower-swimming coarse fish such as perch and eels are preferred to the more agile trout and salmon. Small mammals such as rats and mice, shrews and rabbits are regularly caught, as are frogs and insects at certain times of year.

In some of the limestone lakes and rivers, the freshwater crayfish forms a major part of the diet of both mink and otter, especially in summer. One of the largest invertebrates, it grows up to 4 inches (10cm) in length and looks just like a tiny lobster. Because it likes to hide under stones and is quite slow-moving, it is probably easy prey for the agile otter and mink. Instead of laying her eggs on the river bed, the female crayfish carries them around attached to her body where they eventually hatch into miniature crustaceans. It is known that the crayfish populations in a number of midland lakes have declined recently owing to a parasitic fungus which, it is thought, was introduced to Ireland on fishing gear.

The deep, acid waters of the Upper Lake at Glendalough, County Wicklow reflect the glacial origins of this mountain lake. Such waters are poorly buffered against acidification which may originate from sulphur dioxide pollution in the air or from forestry plantations.

An introduced fish, the roach, is known to be causing serious harm to freshwater lakes throughout Ireland and may well be partly involved in the complex puzzle of Lough Erne. Roach were unknown in Ireland before the late nineteenth century when they were accidentally introduced in rivers in Counties Cork and Tyrone. Coarse anglers are known to use the roach as live bait for the larger predatory pike, and the surplus bait is often discarded. There has also been deliberate stocking of some waters by coarse anglers and, as a result, roach have spread rapidly throughout all the major catchments in the country. They mature earlier than most of the native fish, and females can produce an enormous number of eggs. The huge populations of young roach which result can seriously deplete the invertebrate food resources in a lake or river and threaten the balance in the complex food webs of these fragile ecosystems. Roach will also readily interbreed with other closely related fish such as bream and rudd, producing hybrids with some characteristics of each species. It is likely that a number

of other coarse fish in Ireland are also human introductions, as after the last Ice Age few freshwater fish were able to cross from the European continent before the land bridge with Britain was submerged by sea water. The pike, which lies in wait in many a weedy shallow waiting to pounce on passing fish, is also one such introduction. There is no name for this species in the ancient Irish language and its modern Irish name, *gailliasc*, literally means foreign fish.

Since the 1950s, coarse angling has become one of the fastest-growing water sports in Ireland. Its value to the tourism industry is substantial, especially in the north midlands which have plenty of uncrowded lakes but little spectacular scenery. Unfortunately, this area also has a high concentration of intensive pig farms, and the disposal of slurry in an area with poorly draining soils has led to some of the worst cases of lake pollution in the country. Excessive enrichment leads to massive algal growth and the development of a 'green soup' which removes all the oxygen from

A turlough on the edge of the Burren at Coole Park, County Galway. These temporary lakes dry out in summer and fill again in winter as the water table rises from the limestone rocks below. These fluctuating conditions create a temporary habitat for some unusual plants and animals.

Mute swans will nest almost anywhere near water. The material for the large nesting platform was gathered by the male (cob) and arranged by the female (pen). The incubation period which lasted for about 35 days was shared by both birds. The newly hatched cygnets will leave the nest in a day or so and follow the female around the margins of the lake.

the water. Lough Sheelin in County Cavan, famous as one of the best trout angling lakes in Europe, was grossly polluted during the 1970s and early 1980s. This happened as a result of seepage into the lake and streams of nutrients contained in the pig slurry. In recent years there has been a considerable improvement in the condition of Lough Sheelin with the introduction of a scheme to remove excess pig manures from the catchment, and anglers are once again seeing the large wild trout for which the lake has been so famous. A major spawning stream-enhancement programme, carried out by the Central Fisheries Board, has helped to increase the population of young fish. In 1992 and again in 1993 there were excellent hatches of mayfly, for the first time since 1971, which is a clear indication of the extent of recovery of natural ecological conditions. However, Lough Sheelin is continuously on a knife-edge as periods of very heavy rainfall can increase the input of phosphorus running off the land. Large amounts of phosphorus may also be trapped in the sediments which can be recycled at intervals, promoting the rapid growth of algae.

No Irish lake, however small, would be complete without its mute swans, upending in the shallows to reach the rich growth of water plants which sustain this, the largest of the Irish birds. The nest is a massive platform of reed stems and other plant debris, often built in the shelter of a reed bed at the water's edge. It would be difficult to camouflage such a big nest, but the adults are large enough to chase off a marauding predator such as a fox. Lowering his head and spreading his substantial wings, the male (or cob) swan makes repeated aggressive charges which are usually enough to scare off even the hungriest of intruders. As they uproot water plants from the soft lake sediments, the swans take in small particles of sand and grit which are retained in their gizzards to help in breaking down the food. Amongst the natural grit there are sometimes tiny lead weights, discarded by coarse anglers when their lines become tangled in weed. In Britain thousands of swans annually have died from lead poisoning due to angling 'litter', but research in Ireland shows that death from this cause is still a rare occurrence. At one popular coarse-angling lake, the Cork City Lough, half the swans sampled had high levels of lead in their blood. Lead poisoning, though not sufficient to cause death, may affect the ability of the birds to breed successfully. It could also be one of the factors which makes so many mute swans collide with overhead cables, by far the most frequently recorded cause of death. Perhaps, like drunken drivers, they are unable to make the last-minute change of direction to avoid a crash.

The mute swan population in Ireland must be at saturation point because the birds breed on almost every stretch of open water with sufficient feeding from coastal estuaries to old mill ponds and inland waterways. On the many disused canals in the midlands there is barely enough water for the swans to use as a landing strip; nevertheless, they build their nests in the dense bankside vegetation. In the early nineteenth century, when the Royal and Grand Canals linked Dublin to the River Shannon, these were busy thoroughfares with horse-drawn barges carrying great quantities of coal, turf, potatoes and beer. By the mid-nineteenth century the railways were already taking over from the canal boats and a long slow decline set in. Without the regular traffic nature began to reclaim some of the least-used waterways such as the Royal Canal between Mullingar and Longford and the Ballinamore–Ballyconnell canal between the Shannon and the Erne. Today, reeds grow along the banks and floating water plants fill the channels. The old towpaths have been colonized by willow and alder trees whose long trailing branches dip into the water, providing floating nest sites for moorhen and mallard. The still water, held in by long-closed lock gates, provides ideal conditions for dragonflies which dart amongst the vegetation, the sunlight flashing on their gossamer-like wings.

The development of these linear strips of wetland habitat winding across the central plain of Ireland allowed a number of plant species to spread from the midland lakes and the Shannon Valley into eastern counties such as Kildare and Dublin, which have little natural open water. Similarly, some species of invertebrate animals such as freshwater snails and water beetles are now mainly known in eastern Ireland from the disused canals, especially since many of the important river systems such as the Boyne have been damaged by arterial drainage. The canals provide a place for quiet recreation, for the coarse angler sitting among the reeds and for the walker on the old towpaths. In recent years a movement has developed to restore the disused canals to navigation and, while the prospect of boatloads of overseas tourists is welcome to many of the job-starved communities of the midlands, it will almost certainly mean extra disturbance for wildlife on these quiet midland waterways.

Travelling one October day from Dublin to Galway, across the heart of Ireland, I decided to take a short walk before I reached the west coast. At the

A four-spotted chaser dragonfly (Libellula quadrimaculata) *dries its wings in the sun. These broad-bodied insects fly around ponds, lakes and boggy pools in mid-summer, sometimes hovering and flying in circles as they chase after their insect prey.*

village of Craughwell, within a few miles of Galway Bay , I left the main road and threaded my way down narrow winding lanes between endless walls of grey limestone blocks. After a few miles the road ended in a muddy track, and I left the car to walk along the shore of a wide expanse of shallow water. Away in the distance I could hear the trumpeting calls of whooper swans recently arrived from Iceland. Raising my binoculars, I could see that among the swans there was a flock of Greenland white-fronted geese roosting on a shallow bank at the edge of the lake. Thousands of wigeon swam in large rafts, their whistling calls echoing across the water. Suddenly an enormous flock of golden plover appeared overhead, wheeling and diving as the low evening sun reflected the light from their speckled plumage.

This was Rahasane, largest and most famous of the western turloughs (from the Irish words *tuar loch* meaning dry lake). These turloughs are especially characteristic of the drift-free areas of Carboniferous limestone in the western counties of Clare and Galway but they occur over a wide area of the low-lying midlands. In this region most of the drainage is below the ground surface as the limestone forms a honeycomb network of underground caves and streams. In summer, the water table retreats down into mysterious-looking 'swallow-holes' in the rock and the turloughs become wide grassy areas. Wandering across them are herds of cattle, sheep and horses, unrestrained by fences or hedges. Robert Lloyd Praeger wrote in *The Proceedings of the Royal Irish Academy* (1932) that 'the vegetation of the turloughs is usually nibbled to the last leaf – often much more closely shorn than could be done by a lawn-mower'. He was also the first to point out the distinctive plant life of these seasonal lakes. The blackish moss *Cinclodotus fontinaloides,* which grows on boulders and on the bark of hawthorn and blackthorn bushes around the edge of the turloughs, provides a convenient marker for the upper limit of normal winter flooding. The green moss *Fontinalis antipyretica,* which covers much of the turlough floor, seems to require longer periods of submergence and prefers the sides of boulders to the tops. Some of the tiniest flowers also show a zonation around the turloughs, the rare fen violet growing in the lower, wetter soils whilst the various species of dog violet grow around the upper parts and in the adjoining woodland and scrub. Only very low-growing plants such as silverweed can survive the heavy summer grazing, but around the upper edge of some turloughs, such as the one at Mullaghmore in the Burren, yellow-flowering bushes of shrubby cinquefoil provide a blaze of colour in the early summer months.

The constantly changing water levels in the turlough do not provide very stable conditions for animal life, but freshwater shrimps are able to survive through the summer as eggs in the mud, to hatch again when the water seeps from the rocks below. In 1974 a rare species of fairy shrimp, *Tanymastix stagnalis*, previously unknown in Britain or Ireland, was seen in large numbers in Rahasane Turlough. It grows over one-third of an inch (1cm) in length and moves incessantly through the shallow water with a rhythmical beating of its body. It was suggested that this creature might have been introduced to Ireland as eggs, carried in mud on the feet of a migratory bird or on the boots of a visiting wildfowler. The fairy shrimp has since been found in several other turloughs in the Burren and may well form an important, though transient, food source, for breeding birds in some of the turloughs.

One of these unusual lakes, Lough Funshinagh, in County Roscommon, was once described by the ornithologist George Humphreys as Ireland's premier breeding haunt of aquatic birds. While it has some features of a turlough, such as the swallow-holes, it never dries out completely and has a large reed bed in the centre. As well as the ten species of ducks recorded during the breeding season, Humphreys and his associates found the largest known colony in Britain and Ireland of the rare black-necked grebe nesting here. First discovered in 1918, the colony grew to an estimated 300 pairs in 1932 but declined thereafter as summer water levels became increasingly unreliable. There are no recent records of breeding at all. I have often walked on the summer grassland of a turlough accompanied by the mewing calls of lapwings, circling overhead. Occasionally, I have heard the distinctive trill of a dunlin and I suspect that these secretive waders are much more widespread as breeding birds on the surviving turloughs than is generally known. Unfortunately, many of the former turlough habitats have been lost as a result of arterial drainage carried out by the government since the 1940s.

4

BOG AND FEN

Nothing can surpass the exquisite colouring of the Errif Valley.
Over the dark peat waves the white-plumed cotton grass; brown heather,
too early yet for the warmth of its full bloom, clusters round great boulders
and climbs up the hillsides. Green banks slope away from the river,
losing their emerald brightness amongst patches of darker-tinted bracken,
and bog-land that looks black by their sides. The mountains, too!
What pen could describe, what brush portray them? Peaks that catch the
fierce blaze of sunlight, and flash back in full reflection; hollows
in which shadows lurk, as if they held their own secrets
in everlasting silence.

Joseph Adams,
The Angler's Guide to the Irish Fisheries, 1923

Connemara landscape. A patchwork of
small fields divided by stone walls contains
many surprises such as this wet meadow
and flowering purple loosetrife
(Lythrum salicaria).

A close-up view of Cladonia, *a lichen which grows on peatlands. The cups at the end of the tall stalks bear the spores which are carried away by the wind.*

It would be easy for anybody to make an entire film about what is to be seen during a day spent on a peat bog. I especially like the variety of habitats and the mixture of wildlife which can be observed on the blanket bogs of the west coast. These are the peatland areas which run from the mountains to the sea and where there is a whole assortment of bog pools, streams and lakes. The dramatic and colourful changes in light and mood, which often occur within minutes, have attracted artists down the ages to try to create their own impressions of these fascinating wetlands. Their finished work becomes a magnet for other people to come and see the wild beauty of the area for themselves.

I remember spending a day on a Connemara peat bog with the well-known wildlife artist Richard Ward. He was painting a back-drop of peatland on to his canvas to which he would add specific mammals or birds at a later stage. Richard was particularly interested in the attractive lichens which he noticed growing on a section of an old cutaway turf-bank. These pale-coloured *Cladonias* with their spore-producing red tips made a lovely contrast against the dark background of peat. At this point Richard wanted to add some heather growing above the bank to the picture. As he moved closer to look at the flower formations, a startled meadow pipit flew out from her hiding place and Richard noticed a tidy little nest with five finely mottled brown eggs concealed at the foot of the bush. Just above this vacated grassy spot another colourful creature remained absolutely still, apparently undisturbed by all the commotion. It was an emperor moth with large eye-spots on all of its four wings, sunning itself on one of the heather sprigs. The day continued in this vein, both of us discovering more hidden treasures wherever we looked. The experience seemed like a whole series of 'look-and-find-out' lessons on the peat bog!

For centuries, the bogs of Ireland were regarded as waste places – lonely, treeless expanses useful only for rough grazing and the cutting of fuel. Nowadays, we recognize the peatlands as one of the unique features of the Irish natural heritage. In fact, at one time no other part of Western Europe had such a high proportion (about one-sixth) of its landscape covered by peatland. Today, owing to drainage, peat extraction and commercial developments, less than one-fifth of the original area remains. Our living peatlands not only provide habitats for unique communities of plants and animals but also hold the key to the past, from the continuous record of past vegetation preserved in the microscopic pollen grains to the archaeological clues to our human history. The international value of the intact Irish peatlands became very clear to me on a visit to the Netherlands several years ago, when I was taken to see the last sad remains of the Dutch bogs. By the middle of the twentieth century almost all these peatlands had been used up and the government of the Netherlands spent £33 million on efforts to restore the last few intact sites. It now costs the Dutch people £250,000 annually to keep these peatlands growing. It will take a very long time to gauge the actual success of this restoration programme. We are fortunate in Ireland that we still have peatlands which are growing without the help of such a life-support system, but the number of undamaged sites is reduced each year as the pressures for development overwhelm efforts for conservation.

Peat is mostly water but its solid constituents are largely decayed plant remains. The waterlogged conditions in Irish peatlands prevent the complete breakdown and recycling of plant nutrients as happens in most soils, hence the dead matter simply accumulates and depths of more than 33ft (10m) of peat are not unusual. Because of the unique anaerobic conditions, anything which falls into the bog is also preserved. This includes the minute pollen grains which are produced by plants and blow about in the wind. By taking a vertical core from the peat, scientists today can count the pollen grains under high-powered microscopes and determine the exact make-up of the vegetation of the surrounding countryside at any point over the thousands of years since the peatland began to form. Such technology was not available to Robert Lloyd Praeger, but he foresaw what was to come when he wrote in *The Way That I Went*: 'the bogs and what they can teach us of the past history of our country are yet to a great extent a sealed book, though they will not remain so much longer.' He was referring to the work of the Danish scientist Knud Jessen, whose studies on the flora history of Ireland 'cast a flood of light', as predicted by Praeger, and inspired the later work of Irish scientists such as Professor Frank Mitchell, author of *Reading the Irish Landscape* (1986).

About 10,000 years ago, after the retreat of the last glaciers which had held the Irish landscape in the grip of ice for so long, there was a return to warmer, wetter conditions. I can imagine that the country must then have looked something like the Arctic tundra does today in its brief few weeks of summer. Within a few centuries, vegetation began to spread back across the landscape, first low-growing shrubby plants which were quickly followed by a succession of forest trees – pine, birch, elm, hazel and oak. On a land so recently scraped bare by the glaciers, the soils were poorly developed and there must have been huge meltwater lakes in the low-lying midlands. The largest of these would have formed in the basin of the River Shannon which now drains about one-fifth of the entire island. But there were other extensive lake systems in the valleys of the Erne and the Bann, which today includes Lough Neagh, Ireland's largest freshwater lake.

Across the midlands these meltwater lakes must have been studded with islands (drumlins) and long ridges of glacial sand and gravel (eskers), looking something like the modern coastal landscape of Clew Bay in County Mayo. The lakes would have been shallow and were fed by mineral-rich alkaline waters which were highly productive. Around the edges, where the water was relatively sheltered and shallow, floating pondweeds and water lilies must have found ideal conditions for growth. As these floating plants

died and sank to the bottom of the lakes, their remains did not decompose completely, because of the lack of oxygen in the shallow, stagnant conditions. Instead, they accumulated and the mass of semi-rotten leaves and stems raised the lake bed near to the water surface. With depths of a yard (1m) or less, the first of the emergent plants such as reed and bulrush established a foothold in the organic mass below. The leaves and flowers of these tall aquatic grasses protruded above the water, and their stems were so closely spaced that they slowed the movement of water between them and trapped any silt which was carried in suspension. Every year their long stems fell over into the water and added to the thick mat of semi-decomposed vegetation on the bed of the lake. With each new layer adding extra pressure from above, any remaining oxygen would have been expelled and the microbial action which causes decay would have ceased completely, allowing the development of a unique material called fen peat.

Today, there are few places where fens are still developing, but one of

Glacial scratch marks on a rock in Pedlar's Lake above the Connor Pass, County Kerry. These show the direction in which the glacier moves as it dragged slowly across the ground during the last Ice Age, some 10,000 years ago.

*Carrigower, County Wicklow.
Many marshes and fens in
Ireland have been drained and
converted to farmland but some
small areas still survive around
the margins of lakes, peatlands
and hilly drumlin country.
They include a rich variety
of wild flowers.*

these is at Pollardstown, near Newbridge, County Kildare. From a distance the fen looks like an area of grassland, but in the centre is a narrow band of open water around the edges of which are numerous streams and pools filled with emergent vegetation. Tall reeds take most of the light, only a few smaller plants such as water mint and water horsetail growing in the shade below. The most intact areas of the fen contain a unique type of vegetation dominated by saw sedge, black bog rush and meadow thistle. As the summer progresses, an abundance of insect life emerges to feed on the fen plants. Colourful orange tip butterflies flit about in the sunshine searching for the pink flowers of lady's smock (or cuckoo-flower) on which they lay their eggs, for the caterpillars are quite selective in their choice of food plant. A close-up look at the broad leaf of a reed reveals a mass of aphids (greenfly). These plant-sucking bugs form the main diet of the songbird population which is swelled in summer by migrants including sedge warbler and grasshopper warbler. Swallows and martins, which breed in the surrounding countryside, hawk over the open water, skimming flies from the surface. The fen is continually fed by a series of calcium-rich springs on the surrounding slopes which prevent it from drying out. In the late eighteenth century the streams on the fen were diverted into two main channels which still act as the principal source of water for a section of the nearby Grand Canal. Originally the fen was nearly three times its present size, but extensive turf-cutting, afforestation and drainage have reduced it substantially during this century. Fen peat is still developing here and, if allowed to continue for long enough, the resulting mat of vegetation will completely fill the remaining areas of open water and begin to grow above the influence of groundwater springs.

Many of the midland lakes today have remnants of fen vegetation around their shallower margins, but the majority of true fens have either been replaced by raised bogs or drained and converted to agricultural land. One tiny area of fenland vegetation survives in the midst of intensive farmland in County Westmeath. Its name, Scragh Bog, comes from the Irish word *scráith* meaning a sward or sod. On peat bogs this sward or top layer was removed prior to turf-cutting and was used extensively on roofs as a base for the thatch. Walking across Scragh Bog is a hazardous occupation because the *scráith* is floating on water and actually quakes beneath your feet. Sedges are the most abundant group of plants here, with the slender sedge dominating the wetter margins and fibrous tussock sedge near the centre. Several orchid species add a touch of colour to the vegetation. The centre of the fen is gradually drying out and is already colonized by willow and birch trees which form a kind of wet woodland called fen carr. Around the watery bases of many of these trees grows the round-leaved wintergreen, a rare and unusual plant with evergreen leaves and delicate white flowers. Scragh Bog is also the habitat of a rare damselfly, *Coenagrion lunulatum*, a species only recently discovered in Ireland. This may have been overlooked before because it resembles two closely related and much more common species, the variable damselfly *C. pulchellum* and the azure damselfly *C. puella*. All of these are small, delicate insects with black-and-blue banded bodies little larger than a matchstick. They fly along the edges of deep pools in the fen stopping briefly to mate on the broad leaves of the bogbean or to lay their eggs into the water.

Scragh Bog is, in reality, a fen in transition, for in its centre there are hummocks of moss which have lost contact with the mineral-rich waters below and are creating acidic conditions on the surface of the bog. This moss is one of the *Sphagnums*, a unique group of species which can vary in colour from green and brown to orange and yellow, some even turning red in the autumn. Instead of absorbing water through roots in the soil like

Bogbean grows in the wettest parts of a peatland with its tall flowering spike emerging from the water. The filigree petals of the flower may entangle insects for a while so that they leave their pollen load to ensure fertilisation of the plant.

most other plants, *Sphagnum* moss can drink through all of its parts, including the leaves and stem. Out of contact with the ground and water below, it depends for all its nutrients on the rainfall which is soaked up and held, as in a sponge, in large numbers of dead cells between the living ones. The absorbent qualities of *Sphagnum* were well known to Irish people centuries ago when the moss was often used to dress wounds. A handful of living moss is really a handful of water with a tiny amount of plant material holding it together. Such waterlogged conditions are quite inhospitable for the micro-organisms which cause plants to decay, and so the layers of dead *Sphagnum* accumulate and build up the surface of the bog.

At various stages over the thousands of years which followed the last Ice Age the vast fens which had filled in the meltwater lakes of the midlands became colonized by *Sphagnum* moss. Fen plants such as reeds were replaced by plants which could survive in the more acidic conditions. The upward growth of the *Sphagnum* hummocks produced dome-shaped masses of peat which soaked up water by capillary action. The resulting raised bogs were like a series of waterbeds – great masses of water, held together by a thin skin of vegetation. Several thousand years ago, a traveller crossing the midland plain would have been forced to stay on the winding esker ridges of sand and gravel to avoid getting lost among the great red bogs. But today much of this raised bog has been cut away and only a few small fragments remain relatively intact. One that I have been lucky enough to see is Mongan Bog, within sight of the Early Christian monastic remains of Clonmacnoise, County Offaly. Walking from the edge of the bog I followed a winding trail, steadily rising until, at the centre of the dome, I had a view across the surrounding countryside. The living surface of the bog is a patchwork of pools, hummocks and flat 'lawns' of *Sphagnum* moss. Around the edges of the pools and on the 'lawns' the white-beaked sedge is mixed with the fluffy white flowers of bog cotton and the yellow flowering spikes of bog asphodel. Conditions on the sides of the *Sphagnum* hummocks become progressively drier, and other plants such as lichens, sedges and heathers are able to colonize. On some of the larger hummocks grows the cranberry with its wine-coloured berries.

The surface of the bog is peppered with thousands of wet pools. Some of them are floored by peat and represent part of the tear pattern on the surface of the bog. Others are shallow and filled with mosses, being part of the *Sphagnum* hummock-pool complex. On the top of the water are various pond-skaters and water crickets, predatory water bugs which skate about on the surface film catching both tiny wind-blown animals and other aquatic invertebrates. Their droppings, along with other wind-borne debris such as pollen, sink to the bottom of the pools where they collect among the mats of algae and peat silt. Feeding on the floor of the pools are water beetles, shrimp-like creatures and the larvae of non-biting midges. There are also tiny hunters below the surface such as the nymphs of the emerald damselfly which are quite fierce predators. They creep up slowly to any small aquatic animal, and then a hinged structure (often called the mask) shoots out from below the head, grasps the victim and draws it back to the mouth. Adult dragonflies, such as the four-spotted chaser, also rank among the most efficient hunters above the bog pools. With strong and direct flight they

whizz about like tiny helicopters, using their outstretched spiny legs to form a net for capturing prey in mid-air. When a victim such as a fly is caught, the snapping and crunching of the dragonfly's jaws may be audible from quite a distance. The dragonfly itself may fall prey to a frog. These amphibians are plentiful in the pools and on the surface of the bogs and they play an important role in transfer of nutrients from water to land.

Around the margins of the bog pools are several strange plants which supplement their meagre supply of nutrients by feeding on insects. These include the sundew with its rosette of small flat leaves, each one fringed by a ring of red tentacles. The centre of the leaf is like a helicopter landing-pad: any insect unfortunate enough to land on one will be trapped by the sticky tentacles which fold over it like the arms of an octopus. Bladderwort also lives in the pools, its long flowering spike held above the surface of the water. Some of the leaves form tiny air-filled bladders which create a vacuum to suck in passing prey. The victim is swept into the bladder, trapped, and later digested with the aid of special enzymes produced by the plant. A strong scent resembling that of rotten meat attracts insects to the pitcher plant, a large red and green, fleshy-leaved plant which was introduced from America. It is a rather invasive species, spreading in dense colonies on those bogs in which it occurs.

Walking through the bog vegetation, I followed some well-marked runs which could have been shared by hares, badgers, otters and foxes, for all are regular users of the bog. With eyes to the ground, I searched for the droppings which would give me a clue to the mammal which had been here most recently. Those of foxes usually turn whitish when they dry out as they are filled with feathers, fur and bones. In the autumn, however, when the

Blanket bog, County Donegal. A thin covering of peat clothes the entire landscape except for rocky outcrops. In eastern Ireland it often develops as heather moorland but in the west the peat bogs are more grassy in character.

The white flowers of cotton grass are indicators of the very wet conditions, often found in old bog cuttings. The underground storage organs of this plant are sought after by the Greenland white-fronted geese which still winter on a number of blanket bogs in the west of Ireland.

foxes feast on bilberries or blackberries, the droppings are black and filled with seeds. At other times of year the presence of shiny black wing-cases in the droppings show that the foxes are feeding on the big ground beetles which run beneath the vegetation. On several occasions I have come across the remains of a kill – a small pile of meadow pipit feathers with the characteristic chewed shafts which show that a fox and not a bird of prey was the predator. Foxes have definite hunting territories on the bog and they probably patrol these every day in search of whatever pickings they can find. If a fox has been along the run recently a foxy odour usually lingers in the air. Like all members of the dog family, foxes mark the boundaries of their territory with scent which is sprayed on to the vegetation in the urine. Like most scavengers, foxes survive at times by feeding on carrion, the carcases of dead sheep being the most plentiful on the mountain bogs. Poor-quality feeding and lack of care, especially at lambing time, cause quite a high loss of sheep on Irish blanket bogs, and this helps to sustain the populations of fox, hooded crow and raven.

In the areas of highest rainfall, in western Ireland, a different kind of peatland has developed directly on the bedrock or mineral soil. In poorly draining flattish areas, *Sphagnum* moss grows where there have been no lakes or fens. The result is a thin blanket of peat which clothes the entire landscape including mountain slopes. In the east of Ireland blanket bogs are confined to upland areas such as the higher parts of the Mourne and Wicklow Mountains, but in the west they stretch right down to sea level.

One of the largest intact areas of lowland blanket bog in Ireland stretches across the south of Connemara from the foot of the Twelve Bens to the shores of Galway Bay. The vegetation of blanket bogs differs from raised bogs in that most of it is more 'grassy' in character, with *Sphagnum* moss confined to the very wet areas. More typical plants are purple moor grass and black bog-rush, with carnation sedge and cross-leaved heath covering large areas. The south Connemara bogs hold a greater number of heather species than any other part of Ireland including several very rare ones such as Mackay's heath and Dorset heath, the latter species being unknown in Ireland except for five plants which grow by the roadside near Roundstone. Robert Lloyd Praeger recalled a meeting of world-renowned botanists on the blanket bog here: 'We stood in a ring in that shelterless expanse while discussion raged on the application of the terms soligenous, topogenous and ombrogenous; the rain and wind, like the discussion, waxed in intensity and under the unusual super-incumbent weight, whether of mere flesh and bone or of intellect, the floating surface of the bog slowly sank until we were all halfway up to our knees in water' *(The Way That I Went)*.

Tim Robinson, writing in *The Book of the Irish Countryside* (1987), has described the myriad of lakes which cover the Roundstone bogs as 'like fragments of a pane of glass flung down and shattered'. By talking to the older, Irish-speaking inhabitants of Connemara he has meticulously researched the correct names of these lakes, such as *Loch na mBreac Geal* (the Lake of the Sea-trout). Many of the lakes contain small, rocky islands covered in woodland. Oak, holly, rowan, yew, birch and willow are all present, although many of the trees are stunted by the strong winds. Nevertheless, they form a stark contrast with the surrounding landscape and suggest the kind of vegetation which originally might have covered the remainder of the bog, had it not been for the constant sheep-grazing, turf-cutting, burning and afforestation.

Many of the lake islands in the Connemara bogs support colonies of breeding herons. Their raucous cries echo across the lake water in spring when the large unwieldy nests of dead twigs are built among low branches, often only a few metres from the ground. The herons fly to and from the coast to feed on the rich pickings among the weed-covered rocks in numerous bays and inlets. One of the islands in the bog looks as though it has been hit by chemical warfare. A colony of cormorants, which usually breed on offshore islands, has used the trees here for nesting and the corrosive effect of the the birds' nitrogen-rich droppings has killed off most of the trees. Only the rotting skeletons of the dead trees remain, surrounded by bare peaty soil, bracken or rank herbs. In June, at the height of the breeding season, the scene resembles an urban slum. The closely spaced nests are surrounded by piles of fresh guano (droppings), eggshells, dead cormorant chicks and half-rotten fish regurgitated by the adult birds. From time to time, human disturbance or the complete collapse of the dead trees forces the cormorant colony to move to a new island. Bracken and gorse recolonize the devastated island, but it may be a century or more before trees will grow here again, so radically has the soil been altered.

Much of north-west County Mayo is clothed in lowland blanket bog, stretching from the Owenduff River valley on the western slopes of the Nephin Beg range to the edge of the sea cliffs between Ballycastle and

Top: A golden plover nesting on mountain peatland with eggs and chicks, just hatched. Within a day or two these wader chicks, whose camouflage colours merge with the surrounding lichens, will have left the nest for the safety of thick vegetation. Most birds are confined to the higher mountain slopes but a few nest on blanket bog near sea level on the west coast.

Bottom: Site of Neolithic stone axe factory at Tievebulliagh, County Antrim. Stone axes complete with wooden handles have occasionally been found preserved in bogland. Polished axe heads made at Tievebulliagh from a rock known as porcellanite have been found in many parts of England and Scotland. The probable date of this stone axe factory which seems to have had a thriving export trade, is about 4,500 years old.

Portacloy. The bog reaches right down to sea level at Bellacragher Bay, near Achill Island, and fringes the shores of Carrowmore Lake with its colonies of gulls and terns. Studies of the bog vegetation by Dr Gerry Doyle and his colleagues at University College, Dublin, reveal a complex of deep peat characterized by black bog rush, purple moor grass, mosses and liverworts. This is dissected by a variety of drainage channels and surface features, including pools, depressions and swallow-holes, which provide evidence of an underground drainage system below much of the bog surface. The grassy nature of the main bog vegetation is a direct effect of thousands of years of burning and grazing which also cause compaction of the peat. By contrast, on islands in the bog lakes, isolated from these effects, there are communities of tall, vigorous ling heather growing with juniper and crowberry. The margins of streams and drainage channels support a more luxuriant growth of heathers, with the bog myrtle adding a delicious scent to the air. The numerous shallow pools and lakes on the bog have a sparse vegetation with scarce plants like water lobelia and pipewort mixed with the more common spike-rush and bog bean. Permanently waterlogged hollows on the bog surface are supplied with a flow of water from the surrounding bog and support both the white-beaked and brown-beaked sedge, often with a thick floating mat of *Sphagnum* mosses.

Walking over the miles of bogland, unbroken except by lakes and rocky outcrops, I hear the distant high-pitched cry of a golden plover. These small and delicate waders occupy widely spaced territories on the wetter parts of the bog but are easy to overlook. A close-up view through binoculars reveals a stunning plumage of gold and black, a speckled back and head with jet-black face and underside. While the female sits incubating the eggs amongst the heather, the male bird stands guard a short distance away on a rock or mossy hummock. If disturbed, he will fly a short distance, raise his wings and fly again to distract the attention of the intruder away from the nest. This behaviour is common to all the plovers during the breeding season.

The origins of the lowland blanket bog of western Ireland are revealed in north Mayo where an extensive network of stone walls and pre-bog fields has been dated to the Neolithic period. Stumps of pine and oak preserved in the bog have been aged by radiocarbon techniques giving dates up to 5,000 years ago. In some areas, around Glenamoy, for instance, much older dates for the start of bog development suggest that there were already extensive patches of blanket bog when the first Neolithic people settled in the west of Ireland. The combination of evidence from radiocarbon dating and the discovery of pollen remains of such indicator plants as bog asphodel and beaked sedge suggests that the bog growth began at different times in different areas. It seems that the clearance of the ancient woodlands, followed by farming activity, caused waterlogging of the soils and peat accumulation.

By the seventeenth century, all but a few fragments of native timber had already been cleared and peat (or turf) began to serve as the major source of domestic fuel. This is still the case in many parts of Ireland today, and the sight of crowds of people hand-cutting turf on the bog in spring and early summer is still familiar in parts of the midlands and west. In the past it provided a break from the routine of farmwork and an opportunity for

Hand-won turf cut from the bog and laid out to dry in the wind. For centuries this labour-intensive method of gathering winter fuel has been practised in the midlands and west of Ireland.

neighbours to meet and work together after the long dark days of winter. Each family generally had its own turf-bank or cutting, but several families might work together at each bank in turn. People worked in teams of three or four, cutting, lifting, wheeling and spreading the turf. Opening up a new bank involved removal of the sod of heather, grasses or moss and the mat of fibrous plant material, below which was revealed the dark, glistening turf, like a moist chocolate cake, but a bit heavier. The traditional instrument for cutting the turf is a *sleán*, shaped like a long narrow spade with a metal wing at right angles to the blade. Slicing vertically downwards, the experienced turf-cutter can lift a clean, rectangular sod of turf from the peat bog and toss it up to the top of the bank where it is left to dry. After several weeks, the family returns to the bog for the 'footing' of the turf. A number of sods are propped into small pyramid shapes to hasten the process of drying before they are built into larger stacks, usually near the edge of a road or track. Over centuries this hand-cutting affected the margins of the bogs which were most accessible to wheeled carts for transport of the hard-won turf. Abandoned turf cuttings still litter the roadsides throughout the midlands and west, and these wet areas are often recolonized by the white flowers of bog cotton or by birch, willow and gorse scrub giving a wooded fringe to the bog.

Sand martins sometimes choose a piece of cutaway turf bank in which to burrow their nesting tunnels. When I filmed a small colony of them for the BBC TV series 'The Natural World', the activity that occurred on the day was most unexpected. I became aware that something was amiss when the

birds suddenly became extremely vocal and began flying to and fro in a very distressed state. A stoat had arrived and immediately began to raid the colony. Being a very agile animal it quickly made its way from the top of the bank into one of the nest-holes. It dragged out a chick and then made its way back on to the bank and disappeared out of sight. Its young kittens must have been waiting nearby, as it was back again in no time to continue the assault. The attack continued until five chicks had been taken, then the stoat disappeared altogether. My guess was that, having discovered this handy larder of food, it would return again the following day to carry out another raid on this convenient sand martin colony.

Today, the majority of turf is cut by machine. On the small scale, the *sleán* has been replaced by a tractor-mounted machine which cuts a deep incision in the bog surface and tunnels through the turf below, cutting out the valuable peat. This is later extruded by the machine in long, sausage-like lines of wet turf to dry on the surface of the bog. While the vegetation on top of the bog remains intact, the tunnels below act as drains and the peat quickly dries out and shrinks, causing an irreversible change in the peatland environment.

The largest areas of raised bog have been harvested by huge machines operated by Bord na Móna, The Irish Peat Board. The surface layers are scraped away and the milled peat is transported by rail to the nearby peat-fired power stations. Instead of the hand-cut rough sods of turf, the modern Irish household is more likely to use peat briquettes, milled from the bogs and compressed into compact slabs which are neatly baled for sale to the

The end of a midland raised bog. Modern machinery can destroy a bog in a matter of a few weeks. Some of the peat is used to fuel electricity generating stations but much is exported and sold through garden centres as peat moss.

domestic user. The upper layers of the bog, which contain a higher proportion of fibrous material, are of special value in horticulture, and huge quantities have been baled and exported as moss peat or compost for garden use. Now, thanks to a sustained campaign against this wasteful use of the bogs, peat-free alternative composts are now available in most garden centres.

Slicing through the bog, large harvesting machines often hit solid obstacles which have lain buried in the layers of peat for thousands of years. These are often the remains of trees such as pine, oak or yew, the tell-tale

signs of burning still evident on the timber. Usually just the stumps and roots of the trees remain, as the prehistoric farmers would have cut and burned the trunks before clearing the land for agriculture. From about 5,000 years ago there was a rapid spread of bog in Ireland in response to a warmer, wetter climate. The bogs were treacherous places for travellers across the low-lying midlands and, from the Bronze Age onwards, wooden *tóchars* or causeways were built across many of them to allow easier communication. At Corlea Bog, County Longford, excavations have revealed a 2,000-year-old timber roadway over half a mile (1km) in length

Wintering wildfowl on a peatland pool. From October to April, undisturbed peatlands provide a vital feeding and roosting place for many ducks and for Greenland white-fronted geese.

and constructed of massive oak planks secured on to parallel pairs of tracks, not unlike a modern railway. Deep down, near the base of some bogs, such as Ballybetagh Bog in south County Dublin, the turf-cutters uncovered the massive antlers of the giant Irish deer which roamed the Irish grasslands in the aftermath of the Ice Age. In early Christian times important treasures were sometimes hidden in nearby bogs to avoid being stolen. A visit to the National Museum in Dublin to see such priceless treasures as the hoard of gold and silver objects found in a bog near Derrynaflan, County Tipperary, leaves no doubt about the importance of Irish bogs in preserving the cultural as well as the natural heritage of Ireland.

In the nineteenth century, vast areas of undisturbed peatland still survived in the midlands and west of Ireland. The larger rivers such as the Shannon snaked a meandering path between great unbroken tracts of raised bogs. In October the skies were filled with haunting cries as V-shaped skeins of white-fronted geese arrived from their breeding grounds in west Greenland via their re-fuelling areas in Iceland. The geese were superbly adapted for feeding among the pools and hummocks of bog mosses. Here they probed for the underground bulbs of white-beaked sedge and cotton grass, which they pulled up with their strong bills. These storage organs of the plants contain a high energy content in comparison to the leaves above ground, and cotton grass still forms an important part of the diet of geese in Greenland. At night or when disturbed, the geese moved to the safety of nearby lakes or rivers where they would roost on the water before returning to the feeding grounds. From the 1940s to the present day, large-scale development of the peatlands has deprived the Greenland white-fronted geese of virtually all their raised bog habitats, and only one or two flocks, such as those in Connemara and Donegal, can still be found on blanket bog. The great majority of the population has now moved to winter on the Wexford Slobs, an area of intensive farmland reclaimed from Wexford Harbour in the nineteenth century.

With the vast majority of the midland raised bogs already damaged by peat-cutting, only a few tiny fragments are still growing and wet enough to merit complete protection. But in recent years the rate of extinction of raised bogs has been twice as fast as the rate of their protection. Only 4 per cent of the original area of peatland in Ireland is earmarked for protection but, at present rates of exploitation, it is predicted that all unprotected raised bogs will have been damaged beyond recovery by 1997. For digging a drain through a raised bog is like putting a knife through the centre of a sponge. With such treatment it will no longer hold water, and the surface begins to shrink and lose its original diversity of vegetation. A small group of enthusiastic individuals, very concerned at the widespread destruction of Irish bogs, called a meeting in 1982 and formed the Irish Peatland Conservation Council (IPCC), to ensure the protection of a representative sample of Irish bogs. In 1991 the IPCC claimed a major success in lobbying, which resulted in an agreement with the European Commission, the Wildlife Service of the Office of Public Works and Bord na Móna (The Irish Peat Board) on a raised bog conservation programme. Bord na Móna also gave a commitment that it would not develop any further sites recognized as areas of scientific interest. The Dutch influence was a major factor in launching a much publicised campaign to save Ireland's remaining peatlands. The importance of conserving Irish peatlands has been recognized by the international community in the Council of Europe's recommendations to member states on peatlands in Europe.

And what of the cutaway bogs, those vast areas of corduroy-like landscape which stretch away to the midland horizon? Dr David Bellamy, among others, has pointed out their great potential for short-rotation forestry, or coppicing, to produce biomass fuel for electricity generation. There are already some experimental plots of fast-growing trees such as willow, alder, birch and poplar at Clonsast, County Offaly. In less than ten years these plots have been colonized by a thriving community of breeding birds, with willow warbler and reed bunting among the most abundant species, so that there is also some potential here for habitat creation. Some cutaway bogs which have been long abandoned, such as those around the south of Lough Neagh in County Armagh, have developed a rich mosaic of flooded pools with gorse scrub and birch woodland around the fringes. Many of the larger areas of cutaway bog in the midlands are kept dry by drainage channels and pumping. If this were discontinued the bog would flood naturally and we could see extensive areas of shallow, reed-fringed lakes return over the coming decades. Such a landscape would be not unlike that which covered the midlands after the last Ice Age and from which the fens and raised bogs originally developed.

5

WOODLAND AND SCRUB

Lá dá dtáinig an sionnach, do bhí ainmhianach cealgach mailíseach, chum
bróg Chiaráin; agus do ghoid iad agus do sheachain an comhthionól agus
do chuaigh sé roimhe dá uamhaidh féin agus do shantaigh na bróga d'ithe ansin.
Do ráidh Ciarán ris an sionnach: 'a bhráthair, créad um a ndearnais an
ghadaíocht úd nár dhea-mhaiseach do mhanach do dhéanamh?
Agus ní rángais a leas súd do dhéanamh, óir atá uisce neamh-mhailíseach
againn ins an gcoitinne, agus atá bia mar an gcéanna.
Dá dtugadh, iomorra, do náduir ort go mba fhearrde leat feoil do chaitheamh
do dhéanfadh Dia dhuit do chraicnibh na gcrann so id thimpeall í !'

– from mediaeval Irish account of
St. Ciarán of Saighir, *County Offaly.*

Love of animals was a characteristic of the Irish saints. St Ciarán of Saighir
(the first resident native saint) is related to have formed his first community
of animals: a furious wild boar came to assist him, then a fox, a wolf,
a badger, and a fawn. Thus he made a little monastery in the forest, amongst the
pagans. When the fox gave way to appetite, and carried off the saint's shoes to
gnaw, the badger brought him back. 'O brother,' said Ciarán gently,
'why hast thou done this theft, so unbecoming to a monk? for there are wholesome
water and food for the community, and if thy nature made thee prefer meat,
God would have made it thee of the tree-bark around.'

George Sigerson,
Bards of the Gael and Gall, 1907

Native woodland, County Wicklow. Most
of the ancient woodland had been cleared by
1600 AD and little secondary growth
survived the demand for fuel as the
population doubled in the nineteenth century.
Today only small fragments of native
woodland cling onto the steep sides of
mountainous valleys.

Whenever I walk through an oak woodland in early spring I try to imagine the Irish landscape as it must have looked and felt all those thousands of years ago when the earliest people arrived on these shores. My favourite time for these visits is during the first hours of daylight and, as I enter the wood along a track edged with bluebells and badger-diggings, I become enveloped by the trees in an enchanting, self-contained world. The wind from the Atlantic rustles the twigs high in the canopy but is reduced to a cool breeze in the aisles between the gnarled tree trunks. Droplets of wet mist seem to hang in the still air or drip incessantly from the tips of the newly emerging leaves. The woodland floor is a mass of fleshy wild garlic leaves which give off their characteristic pungent scent as I pick my way between the spongy, moss-covered stones. This is the most musical part of the day and, even before thin rays of misty sunlight have penetrated the woodland, the first members of a large orchestra have begun the overture to what will become a full symphony of melodious birdsong. This band of energetic musicians includes wrens, chaffinches, robins, blackbirds and thrushes. All these songsters are about to resume the daily battle in which each pair struggles to maintain a corner of this rich and bountiful habitat. Sound recordings which I have made in locations like this, even when replayed years later, bring back the same glorious atmosphere of these delightful woodlands.

Broad-leaved woodland is the natural vegetation cover of most of the Irish landscape. If human settlers had never reached this damp island off the western edge of Europe, it would probably still be covered with woodland right to the tops of some of the highest mountains. Professor Frank Mitchell, in *Reading the Irish Landscape*, has visualized the scene that must have greeted the earliest people in Ireland.

> There would have been magnificent stands of oak, elm and pine, alternating with one another in a coarse mosaic as altitude, aspect and soil conditions dictated, with alder confined to the banks of lakes and rivers, and ash and yew growing on rocky precipices. Many of the oaks probably attained heights of 30 metres with long unbranched trunks and small crowns.

For about 2,000 years this 'climax phase' of Irish woodland, with a mixture of oak–hazel–elm–alder, persisted until it was dramatically changed by what may have been a wave of elm disease sweeping through Europe about 5,000 years ago in a similar fashion to the recent Dutch Elm Disease. The pollen record also tells a story of woodland clearance about this time with the advancing tide of early farmers who must have found a deep and fertile soil undisturbed, except by the roots of trees, for thousands of years. There was extensive burning and clearance of forest using stone tools, followed by a shifting cultivation. The natural fertility of the forest soils was exploited for a few years to grow grasses, cereals and herbs and then abandoned in favour of fresh clearings. The fields were often re-invaded by hazel and ultimately by forest trees, producing secondary woodland which restored the fertility of the topsoil. After hundreds of years the same ground may well have been cleared and farmed again. So I envisage Ireland between late Neolithic and medieval times as a country with extensive areas of hazel scrub, in some places merging with secondary woodland or patches of

Bluebells in flower in May before the woodland canopy has fully developed. Later in the summer, the leaves touch overhead and cast a dappled shade blocking out the rays of sunshine.

original high forest, in others opening out into farmland clearings with small settlements.

Even as late as the sixteenth century many of the lowland river valleys were filled from side to side with secondary woods. The evidence is preserved in the place-names, especially those which include the prefix or suffix 'derry' (from the Irish word *doire*, meaning an oak grove). There are over 1,600 townland names in Ireland which contain 'derry': about a third of all occurrences are in the north midland area between Armagh and Roscommon. (A townland is the smallest division of land in Ireland and was probably the land originally occupied by one family.) In an Act of Parliament in 1612 it was stated that 'passages through the woods of this kingdom' were in many places difficult and dangerous. There is no doubt that the extent of woods was seen as a major problem because they provided refuges for wolves and woodkernes (nomadic armed men of the woods). For political reasons it suited the English Crown to clear the remaining woods which provided refuge for Irish rebels. At the beginning of the seventeenth century the largest and densest woods were in the low-lying wetland to the north-west of Lough Neagh, in the Erne Basin, along the Shannon valley, in the river valleys of the west and south and on the eastern slopes of the Wicklow and Wexford hills. The Tudor conquests of the sixteenth century opened up the country for plantation of new settlers, and from about AD 1600 the commercial exploitation of Irish woods entered a new and final phase. Large trunks were sought for building ships and houses, and a major industry developed with the manufacture and export of oak barrel staves. At about the same time large numbers of charcoal-burning ironworks were established. In England coppicing (or rotational cutting) of woodland was practised to ensure continuity of fuel supply. But in Ireland, with the exception of County Wicklow in the east, coppicing was never established, and the ironworks moved from place to place as the local supplies of timber dried up. The resulting devastation of the native Irish woodlands was virtually complete by the end of the seventeenth century, and an increasingly open, treeless landscape appeared. When Arthur Young wrote his *Tour in Ireland* in 1776–9, he reported that County Galway was 'perfectly free from woods and even trees, except about gentlemen's houses'. By 1841 the population of Ireland had grown to 8.2 million (about twice the present population) and the demand for fuel must have been so great that most of the woods which survived were those inside estate walls and even they had to be protected from robbery. With the Great Famine of the 1840s the population pressure on the landscape was reduced, but the magnificent Irish woodlands were never to return.

Although the Irish countryside has many forests, there are few broad-leaved woodlands to be seen. If ever I fly from London to Dublin on one of those rare days when there is no cloud to obscure the view, I always notice one feature of the rural landscape which, above all else, distinguishes the lowlands of Britain and Ireland. In place of the ordered English patchwork of small woods and arable land, Ireland has a tangled network of small green fields and a winding maze of hedges. Those woods which do survive are confined either to steep rocky gorges beyond the reach of normal farming or to the larger country estates where many generations of family stewardship

have ensured the survival of some historic woodland remains. The best examples of the native oakwoods of Ireland are found on the acid soils of sandstone and granite. In the mountains of Kerry, Wicklow, Connemara and Donegal small fragments of the original woodland cover have held on in deep glacial valleys, among the crags and scree, where the ground was too difficult to exploit for most grazing animals. The dominant trees are sessile oak, often stunted and slow-growing compared with the closely related pedunculate oak which is associated with the more fertile lowland soils.

One of the best surviving oakwoods in the east of of Ireland clings to the steep sides of Glendalough (the valley of two lakes), where it watches over the ruins of an early Christian monastery. Built in the sixth century AD, these ancient stone buildings must have been reached by narrow cart tracks carved out of the woodland floor. Whenever I walk in this particular woodland, there is a magical feeling not unlike the embracing atmosphere of the huge, empty cathedral nearby. The air is quite still and heavy with the smells of damp vegetation after the last shower. High above my head a ceiling is formed by the swaying canopies of the trees, the twigs of each one touching the tips of the next. Below these, in shady corners, are the understorey trees and shrubs like holly and hazel with patches of birch or rowan in open clearings. The shrub layer in Irish sessile oakwoods is usually quite thin because of the heavy shade cast by the tree canopy and the thin acid soils, poor in nutrients. By contrast, the herb layer around my ankles and knees may be quite luxuriant if grazing is limited. Bushy bilberry plants are laden with blue-black frauchan berries in autumn and their tiny round

A badger searches for food on one of its nightly forays in the woodland. Although widely distributed in Ireland, the badger's preferred habitat is in woodland or scrub where the trees provide both shelter and food, and the roots act as rafters for the ceilings of their extensive tunnel systems.

A lichen is a partnership between two organisms – a fungus and an algae. They are highly vulnerable to air pollution because they accumulate sulphur which causes the more sensitive species to die. The presence of these shrubby Usnea *species growing on trees is an indicator of very clean air.*

leaves litter the woodland floor in winter. In damper places, where rushing mountain streams fill the woodland with a constant chatter of noise, the broad leaves and nodding flower-heads of woodrush cover the ground.

A rustle in the undergrowth at dawn tells me that a badger has stayed out late to dig for bluebell roots or to hoover up the big black slugs which emerge on to the woodland vegetation after rain. Signs of their nightly expeditions are everywhere in the undergrowth. Well-worn trails criss-cross the slopes and favourite feeding areas are pock-marked with diggings, and characteristic pits filled with droppings. In the muddy ground by a stream or pool, where the badgers go to drink every night, I find the tell-tale footprints showing the marks of their long and powerful claws. With these digging tools the badgers constantly excavate the stony woodland soil, creating new entrances and tunnels in their underground setts. Badgers are widespread in Ireland, from seaside sand dunes to remote moorland and mountains, but they prefer the cover and relative security which they find in broad-leaved woodlands. In areas where there is no human disturbance, badger families can often be observed during daylight hours. The long periods which I have spent waiting for juvenile badgers to emerge out of their sett have been amply rewarded when the two or three youngsters suddenly appear, followed later by one or both of their more cautious and wary parents. The oldest setts are often beneath the roots of old trees on steep slopes where the soil from generations of digging forms great heaps below each entrance and the enrichment from their discarded bedding supports nitrogen-loving plants such as elder. The setts are frequently near the margin of woodland and farmland so that the nightly forays may include some digging for earthworms and beetles in the fields. Decomposing cowpats provide an irresistible source of invertebrate food but this has brought badgers into close contact with cattle and some have contracted bovine tuberculosis as a result. The badger has been widely blamed as a vector of the disease to healthy cattle. While the mechanisms of such transmission are far from proven, many badger setts in woodland and elsewhere are disturbed and badgers killed unnecessarily as scapegoats.

Many years ago, when I first saw the world-famous Lakes of Killarney, I was astounded by the beautiful vision of ancient woodland stretching from the water's edge up to meet the heather-clad slopes of one of Ireland's most spectacular mountain ranges. These woods survived here because they were part of a large private estate and they are now protected in Ireland's oldest national park. Most of the trees are sessile oaks, but there are also important stands of native yew on limestone rocks and a swamp forest on the edge of the lakes. In the lower parts of the oakwoods the strawberry tree *(Arbutus)* is common. This evergreen tree with its bright red fruit is better known from warmer regions of Europe like the Atlantic coast of Spain and Portugal, but seems to find the mild, damp climate of Killarney much to its liking. The ground beneath the trees is rocky and covered with a spongy mass of green bryophytes (mosses and liverworts), which thrive in the almost constantly moist conditions. Under the evergreen yew trees there is hardly any herb layer or leaf litter and the mosses form a virtually continuous carpet covering the ground. In the oakwoods, pools of shade cast by the dense understorey of holly reduce the variety of ground plants,

The large flowers of Rhododendron ponticum *are a surprisingly common feature of deciduous woodlands and peatlands in Ireland. This introduced shrub thrives in the warm wet climate and acid soils which resemble those of its Mediterranean home.*

but the trunks and branches of the oaks themselves give greater access to light and they are covered with a unique hanging garden of lichens, bryophytes and ferns such as the polypody and Wilson's filmy fern. In spring the air is filled with birdsong as chaffinch, wren, robin, blue tit and great tit all mount a spirited defence of their nesting territories. Killarney's oakwoods, with names like Derrycunnihy and Tomies Wood, hold a breeding-bird community which is similar to those in the Welsh and Scottish woodlands but for the absence of woodpeckers and some of the summer migrants. Pied flycatcher, wood warbler, garden warbler and blackcap are almost unknown in these Irish woods on the fringe of Western Europe, although the tiny goldcrest, with its high-pitched call, is more common here than in British woodlands. The explanation may lie in the small size of the remaining Irish woodlands and the reduced number of ecological niches owing to lack of thick undergrowth and the virtual absence of standing dead timber, which is so necessary for species such as woodpeckers. There are some fossil remains of the great spotted woodpecker which suggest that conditions were once suitable in Ireland for this species at least.

While the felling of trees and removal of dead timber for firewood has had direct effects on the woodland structure in Killarney, the indirect results of human intervention have had an even more important influence. From the 1840s onwards extensive formal gardens were developed by the Anglo-Irish Herbert family on their lands around Muckross House at the heart of the Killarney Valley. This included large areas of lawn sweeping down to the lakeshore, with mature Scots pines and many ornamental shrubs. One of the favourite flowering shrubs was the *Rhododendron*, a native of Mediterranean countries like Turkey, Spain and Portugal. This was also widely planted around the valley to 'beautify' the woodlands and give extra cover for game birds such as pheasants. Since then it has invaded much of the understorey in the Killarney woodlands and threatens their regeneration owing to the dense shade beneath its evergreen canopy. In many other peatlands and native Irish woodlands on acid soil, the *Rhododendron* has virtually replaced the holly understorey and shaded out most of the rich ground flora. In the National Parks, such as those in Killarney and at Glenveagh, County Donegal, one of the major challenges is to control and, eventually, eliminate *Rhododendron* from significant areas of woodland. The work is very labour-intensive, involving chain-saw felling of larger shrubs, burning of the cut material and uprooting of young seedlings to prevent them from spreading into new areas.

An additional problem for the woodlands in the Killarney Valley was the introduction of Japanese sika deer in 1864. In the nineteenth century it was fashionable for the landed gentry to have collections of exotic animals and plants which could be admired by their visitors and, from the original purchase by the Herbert family of one stag and two hinds from Lord Powerscourt's collection in County Wicklow, the herd increased rapidly to the present population, estimated to number over a thousand animals. Although in other parts of Ireland sika have interbred with the native red deer, this population in south-west Ireland has remained genetically distinct and is perhaps unique outside of Japan. Unlike the red deer, which are often

found on the open hillsides, the smaller, darker sika prefer the cover of woodlands, and their grazing of young tree seedlings is also limiting regeneration. As natural predators such as wolves were exterminated in Ireland in the eighteenth century, the main limitations on deer numbers are habitat and human intervention. The threat to woodland regeneration and the real possibility of interbreeding between the sika deer and the red deer has made control of sika deer a high priority for the Killarney National Park, although it is argued by some scientists that the Killarney sika are equally worthy of conservation as a genetically distinct breed. This latter view is further supported by much evidence suggesting that the sika deer in certain Japanese locations may have arisen from hybrid and non-Japanese origins.

In my younger days in County Wicklow, I remember looking in the woods for sika deer without much success. They were easy to spot on open mountains in this area and, as I had often seen their tracks in the deep forest, it was obvious that they were using it for cover. It was in Killarney, years later, that I discovered their secret. Sika deer have two methods of defence. When alarmed, they face the enemy, flare the hairs on their white rump patch as a warning to others and then turn around and run away. The second technique is a very different one and seems to be used when the animal is in cover and feels that it has not yet been discovered. I saw a very dramatic example of this general cryptic behaviour in the mid-1970s when a consignment of sika deer from the Killarney National Park was being shipped overseas. When thirty to forty deer had been captured they were kept in one of the spacious old farm buildings in the Park, where they were

A young sika fawn hidden in cover by its mother, remains motionless as it awaits the return of the hind. First introduced in the nineteenth century, Japanese sika deer, in County Wicklow, have interbred with the red deer. The spread of conifer forests has been of benefit to the sika, who can run for cover to the woodlands whenever danger threatens them on the open mountains.

fed regularly with fresh greenery. The windows in the building were darkened in order to give the animals a sense of security and therefore reduce the risk of panic. But anybody coming to enter the building was treated to a spectacular display of group animal behaviour. As soon as the door was opened, the entire herd, as if at a given signal, flopped down on the barn floor. Was this what made it so difficult to see them in the Wicklow forests in those early days?

One of the most unusual features of Killarney Valley is the presence of native yew woodland over limestone around the shores of the lake. In Ireland's most famous limestone landscape, the Burren in north Clare, woodland is a much rarer feature. In the more exposed areas there is no surface water, little or no soil, and the winds from the Atlantic bend any bushes until they grow almost horizontally. But all the evidence from fossilized pollen grains suggests that the Burren was once covered with climax woodland which was probably cleared in the Bronze Age, exposing

the glacial soils to weathering and erosion by the heavy rainfall. In the eastern Burren, where boulder clay has become trapped in the valleys and beneath inland cliffs, I have found woodland of a quite different kind from that in the Killarney Valley. As I clambered among the twisted stems of hazel and ash, covered in a luxuriant growth of moss, I was lucky to catch just a fleeting glimpse of Ireland's most elusive land mammal, the pine marten. Its fur was a deep chocolate-brown with a distinctive cream bib, but the pale-coloured ears were the most obvious feature in the poor light between the trees. This mainly nocturnal carnivore was probably far more widespread in Irish woodlands, but loss of its natural habitat combined with persecution by gamekeepers forced it to resort to remote rocky places west of the River Shannon. Some ancient Irish believed that the pine martens arrived with the Vikings and that they were the invaders' particular breed of cat. As its Irish name, *cat crainn* (tree cat), suggests, the pine marten is quite at home in tree branches where it often robs nests of their eggs and chicks. On open ground

The oakwoods in the Killarney valley are carpeted with moss-covered boulders, evidence of the constantly moist conditions in these oceanic woodlands.

Occasionally the shy pine marten breeds in a deserted building such as this old cottage, situated in hazel scrubland in the Burren, County Clare. The chimney provides both a convenient, safe entrance and a look-out for the pine marten. Although it is quite at home among trees, the marten is more widespread in western Ireland where scrub is more common than mature woodland.

it darts about with a rapid, zig-zag movement, tracking potential prey by scent. On the eastern edge of the Burren, a large area of mixed deciduous woodland at Dromore surrounds a series of small limestone lakes. Here the local population of pine martens has a truly omnivorous diet, with the menu including earthworms, beetles, frogs, lizards, bees, earwigs, snails, small mammals, birds and their eggs. In season they switch to feeding on berries, nuts and crab apples. With such an adaptable diet, it is surprising that pine martens are not more widespread in the Irish landscape. However, attempts have been made to reintroduce the pine marten in several areas around the country, which, in addition to reafforestation, have helped in the spread of this shy and elusive animal.

The limestone which underlies almost two-thirds of the surface of Ireland produces a soil which is alkaline and rich in plant nutrients. Ash woodland is possibly the natural climax vegetation on such soils, but it has rarely survived in a natural state because ash is a valuable timber and the soils are usually claimed by agriculture. I once visited a good example of a natural ashwood at the Hanging Rock, a vertical cliff of limestone in County Fermanagh. As I scrambled up the boulder clay slopes to the foot of the cliff, bunches of the previous year's ash keys rustled on the trees overhead. These are a favourite winter food of bullfinches which move around the wood in pairs even outside the breeding season. They snap off the seeds with their powerful beaks, sending the empty ash wings floating to the ground. Looking up to the canopy I could see plenty of light penetrating the well-spaced leaves of the ash. The trees come into leaf late in the spring, allowing rich shrub, field and ground layers to develop. Typically the understorey is dominated by hazel, but in places blackthorn and hawthorn may form dense scrub. In bare limestone areas such as the western Burren, the ash is often completely absent: only hazel scrub a few yards high can survive in the exposed conditions. Even this type of scrub can support up to twelve breeding-bird species, however. The melodious notes of willow warbler and robin combine in summer with the more rapid songs of wren and great tit. In more sheltered areas and on deeper soils the ground flora beneath ash–hazel woods is especially rich in species. Great swathes of wild garlic produce a mass of white flower heads. The shapely green spikes of lords-and-ladies attract swarms of small flies which pick up pollen and carry it to neighbouring flowers. Primroses, bluebells and wild strawberries are common, as are a number of orchids such as the early purple, broad-leaved helleborine and common twayblade.

Native woodlands also occur on low-lying areas which are flooded in winter. Where drainage is impeded and the soils are permanently waterlogged, the dominant trees are usually alder and willow; birch is more common on acid soils. In post-glacial times, before fens and raised bogs developed in the river basins and Bronze Age people cleared the woodlands, much of central Ireland may have looked like this. The great floodplain of the River Shannon was probably a maze of winding channels and wooded islands. In the early years of the twentieth century Robert Lloyd Praeger described such a unique area of alluvial forest on the River Lee near Macroom, County Cork. Known as the Gearagh *(an gaoire* means wooded river), it formed an almost 'impenetrable jungle' with a wide network of

interlacing streams and wooded islands. In the 1950s about half the forest was felled to make way for a reservoir and electricity-generating station, and most naturalists thought that the last river forest in Ireland had been destroyed. But a remnant remained at the upstream end of the reservoir and this has now been protected as a nature reserve.

I have walked through this area, but with great difficulty because the ground is wet and there are many deep channels. The islands, by contrast, are relatively dry and covered with a mixture of oak, ash and birch and a shrub layer of hazel and hawthorn. Willows and alders are confined to the wetter ground and the edges of streams. In spring the stream sides are bright with the yellow flowers of marsh marigold, and the islands with wild garlic filling the air with its pungent aroma. In open areas away from the shade of trees the channels are filled with sheets of water crowfoot, starworts and pondweeds. Sheltered waterways in the woodland are an ideal habitat for dragonflies and damselflies which dart among the vegetation landing on the water to lay their eggs. In the Killarney National Park there is also an area of swamp woodland or carr which is among the most extensive in Ireland. Unlike the river forest of the Gearagh, it has actually increased in area over the last two centuries as channels became blocked and open marshes with purple moor grass were colonized by the trees. As alder is relatively unpalatable to grazing animals such as deer, the woodland has survived. The distinctive round female catkins of the alder become hard and cone-like in autumn, and flocks of wintering finches such as redpolls and siskins move through the wood stripping them of the tiny seeds which they contain. I

The Gearagh, County Cork. Most of this unique river forest was felled to make way for a reservoir. When water levels are lowered the stark skeletons of tree roots provide a ghostly reminder of this mixture of swamp and woodland.

Top: A female hen harrier soars past on broad wings. Despite a brief recovery of the population in the 1960s, breeding by these attractive raptors has been limited due to persecution, disturbance and unsuitability of the habitat.

Middle: A woodcock on its nest. The cryptic colouration of the plumage matches perfectly the dead leaves on the woodland floor. This wading bird emerges by night to feed in surrounding fields, probing the soil for worms.

Bottom: The native red squirrel is equally at home in conifer plantations and deciduous woodland. It moves gracefully through the branches, from tree to tree, without touching the ground.

have often become aware of these birds by the constant clicking noise which they make when feeding and the fine 'rain' of discarded alder chaff floating down from the treetops. In winter the lake levels rise and the woodland is flooded but, when the floods recede in spring, a rich field layer of sedges and grasses is exposed.

Many of the woodlands in Ireland today are mixed: native and introduced species, deciduous and conifer. Scots pine was present in Ireland after the last Ice Age but it became extinct with man's arrival and climatic change. Many of the large pieces of timber removed from the bogs today by turf-cutters are stumps of pine which must have been enveloped by the spreading peatlands. Scots pine was again introduced in many large estates in the eighteenth and nineteenth centuries and some of these trees still survive today, such as those in the Coronation Plantation, planted in the 1830s in the upper valley of the River Liffey in County Wicklow. The twentieth century brought the era of state planting but this has been dominated by conifers of North American origin. Sitka spruce forms the largest area, lodgepole pine and Norway spruce being the other most-planted trees. All these produce fast-growing softwood timber but, as the bulk was planted on poor upland soils or peatlands, the quality of the timber is low and the management costs are high. The new forests often replace heather moorland with a dense blanket of dark green trees in serried ranks, unyielding to the contours of the land or the subtle changes in soil. In the early years after the plantation is established, a dense thicket of gorse, bramble and fern often grows between the trees, providing cover for an increased population of small mammals and birds like stonechat and willow warbler. These are all potential food to the upland birds of prey, which may benefit temporarily from their presence. For a short time in the 1950s and 1960s hen harriers increased dramatically in some parts of Ireland, taking advantage of the increased songbird populations and lack of disturbance in the newly established plantations. In one such location, I filmed the spectacular aerial food-pass between male and female harrier over the nest site. This gave me a special thrill as these birds had previously been limited to remote areas of moorland and were seldom seen in the breeding season. The male, with striking grey and black plumage, hovers momentarily on his broad wings, while the female passing below receives the offering in her talons. But my excitement was short-lived, and by the 1970s maturing plantations and increasing clearance and reseeding of marginal hill land left a habitat unsuited to all but a handful of harriers.

Today many of the new plantations are on blanket bogland in western Ireland where hen harriers have never been common. Some upland areas such as the Slieve Bloom Mountains in the midland counties of Laois and Offaly, have extensive areas of mature forestry, criss-crossed by dismal tracks where the sunlight rarely penetrates. But there is wildlife here if you know where to look. I remember one particular spring evening, as the light began to fade, I saw a woodcock perform its curious 'roding' behaviour along the edge of a forestry plantation. Flying high above the treetops, this wading bird of the woods followed a pre-determined circular route with rapid wingbeats and a high-pitched, almost electronic call. I stood quite still in the undergrowth, and within a few minutes the bird returned to follow the same

Rhododendron *in the Killarney valley, County Kerry. Despite its attractive appearance this introduced plant poses a serious threat to the future of remaining native woodlands because the shade cast by its large evergreen leaves prevents regeneration of the forest trees.*

precise route, doing so over and over again. A rustling amongst the leaf litter caught my attention and, with a quick flick of its bushy tail, a red squirrel was gone up a tree trunk and out to the tip of a flimsy branch. I had disturbed it feeding on the ground, and it retreated to watch me from the safety of the trees, scolding with its insistent 'clucking' call. On the ground beneath my feet there were the signs of its feeding activity – discarded spruce cones, stripped down to the core to remove the seed at the base of each scale, or hazel nuts, split cleanly down the middle. The red squirrel is still quite common in Irish woods, whether conifer, deciduous or mixed plantations. There is little evidence that it has suffered from the introduction of the North American grey squirrel at Castleforbes, County Longford, in 1911, as this invader is still largely confined to the north and east of the country. I have watched squirrels during the autumn when they were collecting nuts from a nearby hazel grove. A long row of tall cedar trees provided a safe retreat for them whenever they felt that danger threatened, and regular excursions were made between these conifers and their supermarket of hazelnuts. The squirrels did not carry their valuable provisions up into the branches of their high retreat: these were winter stores to be kept for another time when food would become scarce. The nuts were all buried in the grassy area below the cedars, where the squirrels would find them later, probably more by scent than by memory.

Despite the sad and, at times, neglected history of Irish woodlands, I am more optimistic about their future. Many of the surviving fragments of native broad-leaved woodland are now in the protection of National Parks and Nature Reserves, and sympathetic management is beginning to tackle some of the conservation problems such as the impacts of *Rhododendron* and uncontrolled grazing on woodland regeneration. Whilst the pace of afforestation has been stepped up, there are now clear guidelines for planting which are designed to avoid the worst mistakes of the past such as planting in areas of internationally important peatland. The reversal of the EC Common Agricultural Policy has put a stop to most grant-aided destruction of marginal land, allowing nature to reclaim many areas of farmland as the process of ecological succession moves from grassland to scrub and woodland. There are generous incentives for the planting of broad-leaved woodland, but the long return-time for any investment still makes this a relatively unattractive financial proposition for private afforestation. State bodies and local authorities are increasingly planting broad-leaved trees around new developments such as major roads, industrial sites and urban parks, and these new woodlands may compensate in time for the ageing trees of old estate plantations of the last century. Ireland is still one of the least-wooded European countries but some of the woodland wildlife has found refuge in the surviving remnants, in the hedges and forestry plantations, awaiting a time when the trees will creep out again across the landscape.

6

GRASSLAND AND ROCK

The Burren district is one of the most extraordinary
natural phenomena in Ireland. It lies in the north-western district of
Clare and covers many square miles, a vast outcrop of limestone and rock
only partially covered with earth, and in hilly portions completely
denuded of it. As far as the eye can see there stretches a stony
wilderness partially covered with scrub bushes of blackthorn
and hazel, and patches of grass; but entirely treeless.

Lynn Doyle,
The Spirit of Ireland, 1935

A damp hay meadow in June in County
Fermanagh. As the summer days lengthen the
yellow and pink flowers attract a multitude
of insect life to the meadow.
The lack of disturbance to these soils, and low
applications of artificial fertilizer have
produced a rich community of plants
and animals.

Driving through the limestone country of central Ireland one summer recently, I stopped to have a closer look at a hay meadow which I remembered from years earlier. Walking slowly through the field, I noticed the variety of different grasses brushing against my legs. The stiff, bottle-brush appearance of crested dog's-tail contrasted with the nodding flower-heads of quaking grass. I leaned down to look at the tall, umbrella-shaped flowers of angelica which were busy with swarms of hoverflies and flower-feeding beetles. Down in the grass there was an audible hum as countless small creatures moved about among the plants. From the perspective of a ground beetle, the grasses form a canopy with all the variety and colour of a miniature woodland. Down at ground level, the pink and white flowers of clovers and marsh orchids mingled with the yellows of bird's-foot trefoil and the hawkweeds. Blue butterflies were flitting about in the sunshine visiting their food plants, and away in the distance I could hear the bubbling sound of a curlew hovering over its nesting field.

I remember when, not many years ago, meadows like this were commonplace in the lowlands of Ireland, from the great limestone central plain to the windblown, sandy fields of the west coast. Today they are in decline, reduced almost everywhere by artificial fertilizers, field drainage and competition from the more vigorous Italian ryegrasses. The rhythmical swish of the hand-held scythe has been replaced by tractor-mounted mowing machines and silage trailors. But the old meadows still survive in places where the intensive methods of modern farming have not yet penetrated. In many parts of Ireland I have seen the fragments of species-rich grassland which show how lowland Ireland must once have looked. Towards the end of the last Ice Age, about 12,000 years ago, as the climate began to warm up, there was a short period when Ireland was mainly grassland. The pollen rain which fell on the land and became preserved in peatlands was dominated by the distinctive pollen grains of grasses and sedges rather than by trees, as was later the case.

Traditional farming practices such as haymaking still survive in the poorer soils such as those of Connemara, County Galway. The species-rich grassland is cut whenever the weather permits and when dry, the hay is stacked in cocks, each one with its rain cap firmly tied down against the autumn winds.

On these grasslands, newly emerged from the grip of ice, roamed herds of reindeer and the now-extinct giant Irish deer. The remains of this impressive animal have been found right across Ireland, preserved in the raised bogs or in caves where the deer must have been dragged by predators. The finds are concentrated in counties such as Limerick, Meath and Down, areas which today hold some of the most fertile grasslands in the country. The males had magnificent antlers with a span of up to 10ft (3m) and they stood nearly 6½ft (2m) high at the shoulder. Nothing of this kind exists in Europe today. Impressive though these huge antlers must have been during the rutting season, when size scores highly in the deer world, their wide span would have been a major disadvantage to the deer in any wooded areas. So I imagine that during this period the grasslands of Ireland were extensive. With few large predators other than wolves, conditions must have been ideal for the giant deer, until further climate shifts caused their extinction about 10,500 years ago.

By the time Neolithic hunters arrived in Ireland about 9,000 years ago, the giant deer had long since disappeared and the grasslands had been replaced by broad-leaved forests and peatlands which began to become established in the midland lakes. Trees remained the dominant feature of the landscape until about 5,000 years ago when the first farmers began to make significant clearings in the forest. These new settlers brought with them an animal previously unknown in Ireland, which was to have a dramatic impact on the landscape. These were cattle and, to this day, cattle form a major part of the Irish rural economy.

This phase is represented in the pollen record by another increase in the pollen-values of grasses, plantains and weeds of cultivation such as nettle and dock. A change to specialized milk cattle came at the end of the Bronze Age when the smaller Celtic shorthorn was introduced. The advances which these early farmers made are only now beginning to emerge with the excavation of extensive field systems from beneath the blanket bogs of north-west Mayo. A few years ago, while I was making the television series 'Exploring the Landscape', the presenter, John Feehan, jumped down more than his own height from the surface of the bog into a cutaway patch, where there was a long line of whitish stones, buried by the peat. Before making this historic and dramatic leap, he announced that he was about to fly downwards and back through 9,000 years in time. For here there is evidence of the oldest enclosed man-modified landscape in Europe and one of the most extensive Stone Age remains in the world. The huge network of stone walls and tiny fields which have been revealed bear a striking resemblance to the countryside of today in Connemara and western Donegal. Drystone walls were built in western Ireland to clear the land of stones which would have caused serious problems for the early ploughs. They were also an effective way of confining livestock and preventing them from damaging crops before the harvest. There are many gaps and crevices between the finely balanced stones which allow the wind to pass through, thus providing shelter for the animals without creating eddies behind them.

Stone walls are also a favourite habitat for the Irish stoat, providing this efficient hunter with dens for breeding, as well as cover to use when stalking prey. I once stood in the shelter of a wall to watch a stoat hunting rabbits

and I remember seeing some remarkable behaviour on that occasion. The predator singled out its victim and chased it relentlessly, even to the extent of ignoring other potential catches nearby. The stoat was concentrating so hard that it seemed oblivious to my presence. The unfortunate victim became paralysed with fear and squealed loudly even before it was caught and dispatched with a swift bite to the neck. As the prey is often several times larger than the predator, the stoat may eat its kill on the spot and will be extremely reluctant to give it up even if disturbed. Another time I came across a stoat feeding on a rabbit in the centre of a road. I stopped the car, turned off the engine and watched as the stoat dragged the prey slowly into the verge.

Although there are no weasels here, in Ireland the stoat is widely referred to by the familiar name 'weasel'. On the west coast the stoat is known as *an bheainín uasal* (noble little lady). It was once widely believed that the stoat was a fierce creature which could spit poison if annoyed, and so children were warned to keep their distance from it. It was customary to flatter such an animal when it was regarded with suspicion, by giving it a pleasant-sounding name. This was believed to pacify it and make it act in a more kindly way towards humans. It was a custom that offered far more protection to the animal than any conservation law could possibly do!

The Irish stoat looks intermediate in appearance between the British stoat and weasel. It has a black tip to the tail, as do other stoats, but the line between the dark fur of the back and the white underside is uneven, as in the weasel. The Irish stoat is in fact an endemic subspecies with genetic

Hedgerow in bloom in high summer. The wild, untended nature of most Irish hedges provides an important refuge for many of the native woodland plants and animals which would otherwise have disappeared from the Irish countryside.

characteristics which distinguish it from all other stoats. While nearly all stoats in the northern part of Europe turn white in winter to blend with the snow cover, this is almost unknown in Ireland, where snow rarely lies on the ground for more than a day or two. Stoats are found at all altitudes in Ireland, but as their principal prey, rabbits, are more common in grasslands, stoats are most often seen in lowland areas. The stoats menu also includes mice and birds.

Hedges are today as much a part of the lowlands of eastern Ireland as are drystone walls to the west. On the small country roads near my home in County Wicklow, it is difficult to see into the neighbouring fields because of the tall, unkempt hedges of hawthorn and ash, gorse and holly. They give the appearance of antiquity and are of great interest to the naturalist, but the enclosed landscape of today was virtually unknown in Ireland a little over two centuries ago. Up until about 1750 the rundale or openfield system was commonplace, with clusters of houses known as *clocháin* around which the

crops were grown. Beyond this the land was open and unfenced, and livestock was guarded by herdsmen against wolves which still persisted in more remote parts of Ireland, and to keep the livestock on appropriate grazing. The combination of a rising population and agricultural 'improvements' led to the introduction of permanent enclosure with hedges, and the scarcity of woodland in Ireland today is compensated for in some small way by the number of hedgerows which occur all over the country. They provide an important genetic reservoir for a large assortment of the countryside's flora which might otherwise become extinct. The variety of plants found in many hedges resembles what one would expect to find at the edge of a mixed wood. Mammals, large and small, take advantage of the protective covering these places offer when they want to build a home or to travel under cover from one area to another. Whenever I need to convince myself how important hedgerows are in protecting crops and farm animals from our weather, I compare the relatively slow growth of plants on the

The hawthorn (or whitethorn) lights up the countryside in May with its masses of white flowers. Most Irish hedges are less than two centuries old but the complex network of mature hedgrows now gives the Irish landscape a wooded appearance.

The linnet, a common hedgerow songster. Nesting in small colonies, the linnet prefers the dense foliage of thorny shrubs such as gorse (or furze). It feeds on seeds, moving around in noisy flocks in late summer and autumn.

windward side of the hedge with the much more advanced flora on the sheltered side of the hedge.

By far the commonest hedgerow shrub is the hawthorn (or whitethorn) which grows well in nearly all soil types. The thorn quicks were usually planted into an earth bank or stone-faced bank where they quickly grew to form a dense thorny barrier, ideal for nesting songbirds. As the shrubs mature they produce a heavy crop of berries (or haws) which form the main early winter feeding for a whole range of birds, mammals and insects. October is the time for arrival in Ireland of large flocks of migrant thrushes including redwings from Iceland and fieldfares from Scandinavia and Russia. I have often seen them feeding ravenously on the haws and rising into the sky with loud 'chucking' calls when disturbed. Hawthorn can withstand heavy pruning each year, but when unmanaged, as is often the case with Irish hedges today, they grow into quite tall trees. The mixture of shrubs and trees in the hedges reflects the combination of soil type, climate and history. In the rich lowland soils of the east and mid-west hawthorn is abundant, with a mixture of blackthorn and elder. The hedges are tall and fast-growing, and ash trees are especially common. The timber from the ash tree produces a fine straight grain which is ideal for making the *camán*, or stick, used in the traditional gaelic sport of hurling. The great all-Ireland hurling final, held each year in Croke Park in Dublin, is still known as the 'clash of the ash'. Each *camán* must combine a delicate balance of weight and flexibility for the top players to hit the leather ball, or *sliotar*, the length of the field. The game dates back at least to the days of the legendary Celtic

hero Cuchulainn who, it is said, was so fast that he could hit the *sliotar* away from him and catch it again before it landed.

Many of the hedgerow stands of ash, beech, oak, horse chestnut and sycamore are now reaching maturity, but their uppermost branches still support countless nesting colonies of rooks, which follow the plough. In the more acid soils of the north-east and south-east parts of the country, gorse is frequently an important part of the hedgerow shrubbery and Scots pine is a typical tree. In the limestone country of east Galway and north Clare most of the field boundaries are stone walls sometimes accompanied by sparse hedges of hawthorn, blackthorn and hazel, resembling the natural woodland cover in these regions. On hillsides and in the more exposed south-western counties the hedges are generally low-growing, with gorse and broom as the dominant shrubs giving a blaze of yellow flowers in spring and early summer. On very exposed western coasts in Cork, Kerry, Galway and Mayo the dangling scarlet flowers of fuchsia enliven the hedges, as this introduced shrub from South America seems to prosper in the frost-free conditions of the Atlantic seaboard.

Many Irish hedges have a neglected appearance but they form an important breeding and wintering habitat for birds. The most abundant nesting species are all residents such as the wren, robin, blackbird, chaffinch and dunnock (known locally as the hedge sparrow), while summer migrants such as the willow warbler, chiffchaff and spotted flycatcher make up a much smaller proportion of the bird community here than in comparable areas of farmland in other parts of Europe. It has been suggested that the

A female sparrowhawk with well-grown chicks beginning to moult their downy feathers. The eggs are usually laid in an abandoned crow's nest, high in the canopy of a tree. Small songbirds form the bulk of the diet for this common raptor.

133

mild Irish winters allow resident birds to stake out their territories earlier in the spring than they would in countries with more severe conditions, leaving little space available for the migrants which usually arrive in April and May. By mid-May the hedges are already full of hungry young fledglings and many of the adults have a second brood well on the way. The inexperienced young birds provide easy prey for the sparrowhawk which twists and turns on short, rounded wings as it hunts among the hedgerow trees. This is probably Ireland's most widespread raptor, common in woodland and forestry plantations as well as lowland farmland – a pair of sparrowhawks comes on regular raiding trips to my garden in County Wicklow. The feeding activities of finches and tits are obvious to these sharp-eyed raptors, even from several hundred yards across the valley. Their assault flights are quite successful, with birds scattering in all directions as one or other of these whirlwind attackers plucks an unlucky victim from my hanging peanut feeders. There is a very healthy population of finches in this part of the country, so there is sure to be a good surplus of young birds available in winter. If not taken by predators like the sparrowhawk, some would almost certainly die of food shortage.

At night-time the hunting ground of the sparrowhawk is taken up by the barn owl, one of the more mysterious farmland birds. Its name in Irish, *an scréachóg*, means the screecher, although the barn owl is just as likely to be heard in its roost making a peaceful snoring noise. It is also known locally as *an ceann cat*, meaning the cat's head, which I take to be a reference to the round facial disc of the barn owl and its large, forward-looking eyes. I know a quiet, out-of-the-way place where, on a summer's evening, I can be fairly sure of seeing a hunting barn owl. The first indication I usually get of its presence is the warning cries of blackbirds in their roosts among the bushes. Then a ghostly white shape emerges from the fading light to hover momentarily on its powerful wings above a potential victim. The wingbeats are deep and slow and the dense covering of soft feathers on all parts of its body ensure that the bird makes no sound as it quarters its hunting territory. The best habitats for the barn owl include a significant amount of damp, unmanaged grassland which has high populations of field mice. The hunting expeditions usually follow well-established corridors such as the rough vegetation on the edges of streams, hedges or forestry plantations. Hedgerow trees or fence posts along the route provide an alternative means of 'perch-and-wait' hunting which becomes more efficient in strong winds or rain. The high rainfall and consequent risk of waterlogging of tree nests have forced most barn owls in Ireland to breed in man-made structures. Traditionally the 'white owl' was welcomed around farms as a way of controlling rat and mouse populations. The owls often built a nest among bales of hay or in the rafters and stonework of outhouses. Farmers today usually rely on rodenticides as a means of controlling the pests, and modern farm buildings leave few suitable nest sites for the barn owl. As a result, disused buildings such as old cottages, churches and castles are now more often favoured as nest sites.

Over 95 per cent of the lowland county of Meath in the east of Ireland is improved farmland, whilst in the mountainous County of Donegal, in the north-west, the proportion declines to less than 40 per cent. But in both

eastern and western regions, Ireland is largely a country of grassland. Only in parts of the south and east are the climate and soils suitable for growing cereals, whilst west of the River Shannon the area of crops rarely exceeds 10 per cent. Grass is the cheapest feed for cattle, sheep and horses, and because fodder is sometimes in short supply livestock are often overwintered on the land. In Ireland a pasture usually means grassland which is grazed, whilst a meadow is an area closed off from grazing in the spring, to be mown in summer for hay or silage and possibly grazed again in autumn and winter. Permanent grassland such as this is much richer in animal life than land which is ploughed and sown with intensive crops. The high densities of soil invertebrates in Irish grasslands attract large winter flocks of lapwing and golden plover seeking refuge from colder, less productive lands further east.

In the colder parts of Europe, the need for winter fodder can mean the difference between life and death for farm animals, but the milder Irish climate often allows livestock to be overwintered on grass. As a result, the practice of haymaking was a late introduction to Ireland. There are no early literary or archaeological references to it, and it was the sickle, not the scythe, which was the traditional tool of the harvest. But with increasing livestock numbers in recent centuries hay-making became a significant feature of the farming calendar. The whole family was involved in mowing and 'saving' the hay. They spent the long sunny days turning the new-mown grass and tossing it up on forks to let it dry thoroughly in the wind. Traditionally, the mown grass was coiled around the forearm to form hollow 'laps' through which the wind could pass. As the hay became progressively

Hidden in its meadow habitat the corncrake reveals its presence with a loud 'craking' call. Changing agricultural practises have brought this summer migrant close to extinction in Ireland.

Clonmacnoise, County Offaly. The ruins of an early Christian monastery overlook an extensive area of species-rich meadows on the Shannon callows. Here the corncrake still calls each summer until the weather allows mowing and haymaking in July or August.

drier it was piled into larger and larger haycocks which were eventually carted back to the haggard beside the farm buildings. Here it was carefully stacked and thatched with rushes to keep the valuable fodder dry. The thatch had to be roped on, even with the use of heavy stones at the end of the ropes to hold down the stack against the winter winds.

For centuries past the summer hay meadows would have been incomplete without the distinctive 'crake–crake' call of the corncrake *(an traonach)*. I have heard older country people complain of being kept awake at night by birds calling all around their houses. After one of my films was shown on television, an Aran islander commented on the sequence about the corncrake. He was quite surprised that I had succeeded in photographing the bird craking while it walked around in the meadow. 'Wasn't it common knowledge that the corncrake lay on its back while it craked?' he remarked. The belief in this strange behaviour was not confined to the Aran Islands. Indeed, in some more imaginative minds, the bird not only lay on its back with its feet in the air, it also kept the sky up for good measure!

But there are no corncrakes left in the Aran Islands and I know only a few places where I can be sure of hearing a corncrake today. These are the small farms and fields of north Donegal, the islands of west Galway and Mayo, and principally it is in the great flood plain of the River Shannon, where the corncrake clings precariously to the last of its favoured hay-meadow habitat. There are times when I have stayed out till at least midnight and listened carefully for the unmistakable, almost electronic sound. Some older people have told me that the corncrake is flightless as the birds have a tendency to

Ragged robin in flower during June. This beautiful wetland plant enlivens the hay meadows in the damp soils of lowland river valleys. As summer progresses the grasslands become a sea of pink.

run through the grass rather than fly away from danger. But in fact they are long-distance migrants, arriving here from their African wintering grounds in early May. If the grass is too short at this stage of the season they move into nearby wetlands and drainage ditches, calling to each other from the cover of the deep clumps of yellow iris (or flags). As June progresses, the corncrakes nest in the tall grass of the meadows where they are surrounded by a rich insect life. The downy black chicks hatch in July and are soon mobile enough to be led from field to field by their parents in search of the best feeding. In the days of the hand-scythe, or even the horse-drawn mower, there was plenty of time for the corncrake broods to escape the blades. But the introduction of rotary mowers, on tractors capable of speeds up to 6 miles (9.7km) per hour, spelt doom for the slow-moving birds, and mortality increased significantly. Saving a good crop of hay was never easy in the damp Irish summers, and with increasing farm mechanization in the 1960s many farmers switched to silage which could be made even with wet grass. This began a trend for earlier and earlier mowing in meadows which had been reseeded with vigorous grasses fed by artificial fertilizers, until some fields were producing up to three crops of silage in a season, the earliest being usually cut in May. While these farming 'improvements' gathered momentum through the 1950s and 1960s the corncrake was steadily contracting in range until it had become rare east of the River Shannon. In the mid-1980s, after two disastrously wet summers, the area of meadow in Ireland used for hay dropped to about 40 per cent whilst silage increased to 60 per cent. By this time there were estimated to be less than a

The Esker Riada in County Offaly. This ridge of glacial sand and gravel winds across the flat Central Plain providing dry ground in a landscape of raised bogs and river floodlands. It was an important route for early travellers across the midlands of Ireland. An important source for stones and gravel, few if any of Ireland's eskers remain undamaged.

thousand calling corncrakes in Ireland and the species was nearing extinction in one of its former European strongholds.

But corncrakes still call out in the summer grasslands on the banks of the River Shannon much as they would have done when the early Christian monastery of Clonmacnoise was in its prime 1,200 years ago. The meadows here change colours as spring progresses. Depending on which particular flower is prominent at the time, the overall effect can be a delicate lilac shade when lady's smock is in bloom or an overall sea of pink when the grasslands are taken over by masses of ragged robin. My favourite time of year for visiting these meadows is the spring, preferably when there is little or no wind. This is when the invisible tenants of the meadows can be enjoyed just by listening to the whole variety of mysterious musical messages which they create as they communicate with one another. The corncrake is by far the loudest voice: its habit of moving around while it calls has given it the reputation of being a ventriloquist. Its call, which sounds like an old fishing reel with the ratchet on, is in complete contrast to the much quieter and repetitive 'qui-qu-ic' call of the tiny quail. Meanwhile, the sweetest and most popular of songsters, the skylark, is poised overhead enthusiastically singing its beautiful warbling tune before gradually sinking downwards and then suddenly dropping into the grass. The list of interesting sounds grows as a pair of redshank call to one another, and a snipe, whose mate is already sitting on eggs, creates a drumming noise away above me. It alternates its rapid skyward flight with sharp descents, creating a sound resembling the bleat of a goat which has earned it the Irish name *meannán aerach* (lively kid

goat). This enchanting sound is produced not by the vocal chords, but by the wind vibrating the outer tail feathers as the snipe shoots down towards the meadow.

A pilgrim approaching the monastery at Clonmacnoise from the east would have walked on the Great Road (*Eiscir Riada*) which winds its way between the raised bogs and the river. This long gravel ridge still provides a safe route across treacherous ground, and the term 'esker' is now widely used internationally to describe these glacial features. They were formed by meltwater rivers flowing in tunnels beneath the ice cap during the last glaciation. The water carried with it a load of sand and gravel which was later dumped on the floor of the tunnel. When the ice cap finally melted, the filled tunnel was left as a long ridge of sand and gravel winding across the countryside. Originally the eskers were covered with woodland of oak, ash, hazel and elm, but these were gradually cleared away by early farmers and replaced by grasslands with up to eighteen different grass species. Because the esker soils are formed of free-draining, lime-rich sand and gravel, they support a meadow community similar to the chalk downlands of southern England. Colourful flowers such as cowslip, devil's-bit scabious, bird's foot trefoil and white dog daisy abound on the steep slopes of the eskers, and on warm sunny days the air is full of dancing butterflies such as the common blue. Amongst the vegetation there are subtle indications of the antiquity and lack of disturbance in these pastures. The delicate green-winged orchid opens its purple flowers in early summer, and numerous anthills have survived here because of the difficulty of ploughing or cutting

Female kestrel at the nest on a cliff ledge. These common falcons often nest in ruined buildings and hunt over rough grassland. With fanned tail feathers and quivering wings they hover in the air, searching the ground below for the slightest movement of a mouse or shrew.

hay on the steep slopes. The only disturbance comes from grazing cattle and from quarrying, as the sand and gravel are valuable building materials and their sale helps to supplement the meagre income from farming in these boggy midland areas. On a hot summer day I once watched a kestrel hunting along the steep slopes of a midland esker. It flew a short distance with eyes quartering the ground, then, sensing a movement in the grass below, hovered motionless with fanned tail and quivering wings. From the summit of the esker ridge I, too, had an unbroken view, far and wide across the central plain of Ireland.

Many of the roadside verges in Ireland are still bright with wild flowers but there was a time when even cereal crops included a colourful mixture of weeds such as the tall red flowers of corn cockle and wild poppy. The variety of native flowers which grew among the corn attracted a range of pollinating insects and the field was a real living community. With better seed-cleaning techniques and the use of herbicides many of these arable weeds of cultivation declined dramatically throughout Europe after the 1940s but

they probably survived longer in Ireland where farming was slow to modernize. When the first *Irish Red Data Book on Vascular Plants* was in preparation in the 1980s, two arable weed species, cornflower and darnel, were considered to have become extinct in Ireland. The beautiful blue cornflower is a weed which was once common in corn and flax crops, whilst darnel was an extremely common grass of cultivated fields and waste ground. In a dramatic discovery in 1988, both species were found alive and well in the Aran Islands, off the coast of County Galway. Almost all were growing in fields of rye, traditionally grown as a hay crop or for the value of the straw for thatching buildings. The rare grass darnel was even seen flowering in the older, little-tended thatched roofs. By sheer chance these rare plants have survived in Ireland because of the preservation of traditional farming methods.

Rye is one of the hardiest of all cereal crops and was once important throughout north-west Ireland where it produces a good crop even on infertile, acidic soils. Tim Robinson, in his book *The Stones of Aran* (1986),

Traditional farming on the Aran Islands. Potatoes and other vegetables are grown on 'lazy-beds' where the sod under the ridge is not dug, but the bed is built on top of the grass using soil dug from the trenches. This system prevents the beds becoming waterlogged in the high rainfall conditions of western Ireland. These fields were created by generations of islanders who mixed seaweed from the shore with dune sand to produce soil on the bare limestone.

describes an old man threshing rye, 'whipping each fistful of stems across a wooden bench so that the grain fell on to a spread sheet and the chaff went glimmering downwind'. The threshing was done by hand. A similar activity which I observed in Carraroe in Connemara was included in my film on Ireland for BBC TV's 'The Natural World' series. The grain on that occasion was oats which Pat Ó Cualáin was using to feed his hens and geese. At a time when all these tiny cornfields in Connemara were being cut by hand-sickles, the straw was undamaged and therefore widely used for thatching the roofs of local cottages and outhouses. The straw which is disgorged by modern harvesting machines is quite useless for the traditional craft of thatching.

Looking south from Connemara across the waters of Galway Bay, the great, grey, rocky landscape of the Burren looms up like a stranded whale. From a distance the stepped limestone hillsides appear to be quite bare but in closer view the plateau is dissected by fertile lowland valleys which are filled with species-rich calcareous grassland. I once swam ashore here after a diving expedition on the coast of County Clare. There is a certain strange feeling of enjoyment in coming ashore and contrasting life underwater with life on dry land, especially if one is surrounded by the magic of the Burren on a warm, sunny day in spring. A profusion of sea pinks and sea campion grows on the rocks, barely above and beyond the splash zone. Even before I had left the edge of the sea, I could see a sample of what the Burren has to offer from its treasure-chest of nature. Carpets of bird's-foot trefoil and smaller patches of wild thyme and saxifrage are sprawled around the grassy

The common blue butterfly is widespread in coastal and limestone regions where bird's foot trefoil, its main food plant, grows. The Irish butterfly is larger and a brighter blue than the British. The females are dusky brown with orange spots on the wings. The adults are on the wing from June to August.

areas between the rocks. The six-spot burnet moth, which flies during the day, is conspicuous in its fine black and red costume, especially during mating when dozens of the moths seem to concentrate their energies around the wild thyme. Later they will lay their eggs on the leaves of bird's foot trefoil. Walking inland across the more exposed areas of weathered limestone I was leaping across numerous deep fissures (grikes) in which grow a profusion of colourful plants. The unspoken rule among many of the Burren flowers is 'keep your head down in the trenches'. Every grike and hollow has been taken advantage of by the plants. When I looked a little more closely into the grikes I could see rare and delicate plants like maidenhair fern sheltered from the wind. As the summer progresses from May to August, a bewildering array of wild flowers such as spring gentian, mountain avens, bloody cranesbill and early purple orchid follow one another in rapid succession. The plant communities of the Burren are unique in Europe because they include both southern or Lusitanian species and northern or Alpine plants, all growing together close to sea level. The frost-free conditions and the absence of shading by trees have allowed this remarkable assemblage to survive here, although pollen analysis shows that the Burren was once covered with woodland, like most other parts of Ireland in the period immediately after the last Ice Age. The wealth of archaeological remains in the Burren confirm that this now impoverished area once supported a thriving human population. Woodland clearance for farming in the late Neolithic–early Bronze Age started the process of soil erosion from the Burren hills. Large quantities of soil were washed into

The cuckoo is widespread throughout Ireland in summer. The earliest call of the males, when they arrive from Africa (usually in late April), is the cause of much correspondence in the newspapers. In late summer single juveniles such as this one, are easily seen as they wait for their 'foster parents' to provide food.

underground caves where they can now be accurately dated. Some of the old stone walls which criss-cross the Burren landscape are also thought to date back to the Bronze Age, giving an unbroken record of farming over about 4,000 years.

Many times, when I have set out to photograph the stunning wild flowers in the Burren, I have been equally attracted by the amazing diversity of insects which live amongst them. Perhaps most impressive to the summer visitor are the butterflies which include many species that are rarely seen in the rest of Ireland. The typical limestone grassland species are common blue, small copper and small heath, their caterpillars feeding on bird's foot trefoil and various grasses. Rarer species include small blue, dingy skipper and grayling, while the bright yellow brimstone butterfly is found wherever its host plant, buckthorn, grows. Various fritillary butterflies are here too, including the scarce pearl-bordered and marsh fritillaries. After dark the wild flowers attract hundreds of moth species including the beautiful Burren green moth which was unknown in Ireland or Britain before its discovery here in 1949. In all, the Burren boasts more kinds of butterfly and moth than can be seen in any other part of Ireland. In most years the resident species are supplemented by millions of migrant insects blown in on the warm winds from the European continent. Peacock, red admiral and painted lady make an annual appearance, but the star of the summer show is the beautiful clouded yellow butterfly which comes only infrequently.

The wide open landscape of the Burren offers endless opportunities to follow the progress of another summer visitor, the cuckoo, as it flies from one look-out point to another, watching for the moment when it can lay its egg in some unwary bird's nest. The cuckoo, as a harbinger of spring, seems to feature far more in Irish traditional love songs than does the swallow. But, then, the kind of music created by the cuckoo is far more obvious in the countryside than that of many other birds. While most country people have heard a cuckoo call, few can claim to know what the bird actually looks like. In appearance the cuckoo is not unlike the male sparrowhawk but it has very pointed wings, a rather long and rounded tail with white-tipped feathers, and a small head. Its upper parts and throat are blue-grey and its underparts whitish with dark bars. Unlike the sparrowhawk, its flight is direct and usually low above the ground, where it is often chased by other birds. The male bird makes the distinctive 'cuc-coo' sound, whilst the female has a long bubbling call, and both birds have variations to their particular pieces of music. In Ireland the meadow pipit seems to be a favourite choice as foster-parent for the cuckoo's single ravenous chick, a factor which has earned it the Irish name of *banaltra na cuaiche* (the cuckoo's nurse). But there is a long list of birds which have been chosen to carry out this extraordinary duty. The most recent example I came across was in a robin's nest which the birds had built on the ground, tucked into a clump of grass. At first there had been five eggs in the nest but one of these had been replaced by one of the cuckoo's own eggs. When the family of robins hatched out they were gradually shouldered one by one out of the nest by the young cuckoo, who by now had all the food and attention to itself. I watched the robins work overtime as they stuffed more and more food into a large beak which never seemed to stop calling for extra helpings of worms and caterpillars. Towards the end of three weeks there seemed to be only one very delapidated robin feeding the cuckoo. The juvenile bird was now ready to fly and had grown so big that the poor foster parent would often stand on the adopted youngster's back to feed it. I had no way of knowing what happened to the second robin – possibly it took early retirement at the thought of it all !

7

MOUNTAIN
AND MOOR

*You can set foot on the heather six miles from the centre of Dublin,
and save for crossing two roads, not leave it til you drop down on
Aughrim, thirty miles to the southward as the crow flies, keeping all the
while along the granite backbone of Wicklow. Or if you take the
Military Road, it will lead you along the range to the same place by a
more picturesque route past Lough Bray and Glenmacnass waterfall,
rising twice to 1,600 feet and dropping into deep valleys, giving
you views of Glenasmole and Glencree and the upper Liffey
and Glendalough and Glenmalure all places to be not glanced at,
but explored at leisure, for they are lovely and interesting.*

Robert Lloyd Praeger,
The Way That I Went, 1937

*The Gap of Dunloe passes through the
Macgillicuddy's Reeks. To the left of the lakes
are Tomies Mountain and the Purple
Mountain. The walk along the ridge above
the Gap, according to the nineteenth century
naturalist H.C. Hart, was 'the grandest bit
of mountaineering to be met with in Ireland'.*

One June morning, I went for a long walk in the Wicklow Mountains in the east of Ireland, to find a herd of deer that I had not seen for some time. It was a fine sunny day, and some people from the city were already out cutting turf to make the best of the dry weather. Bog cotton was in flower everywhere, its fluffy white heads waving in the wind and reflected in the waters of a dark bog pool. My legs brushed against the heather as I walked along the narrow sheep track and this caused a variety of moths to flutter upwards for a moment or two before landing again. With a great whirr of wings, a pair of red grouse took off, flying over the heather until they disappeared beyond a turf bank. When I moved off the path to catch sight of an unusual moth, I disturbed a hare which jumped and bounded away from me, but when I did not follow it stopped to look at me. I discovered the form where it had been resting – a small, comfortable hollow in the grass. I could feel with my hand that it was still warm. As I climbed over the ridge a curlew was calling somewhere in the distance, probably warning its mate that there was an intruder on the mountain. For me there is no more typical sound of mountain bogland than the beautiful liquid whistle of the curlew. Then suddenly I saw a movement through my binoculars. Twelve pairs of velvet-covered antlers were poking out from the heather as the whole herd of deer lay resting in the morning sun. All was well with the mountain herd and I turned for the long walk home.

The mountains of Ireland have one outstanding feature – lack of people. I have often walked for a whole day and seen only one or two hardy souls – the occasional sheep farmer with his dogs, a couple of hill walkers far from the nearest road or a lone fisherman hoping for a trout in a mountain lake. About a quarter of the island of Ireland consists of upland-type habitats, with the majority of this area less than 30 miles (50km) from the sea. In western Ireland blanket bog, a habitat usually associated with uplands, reaches right down to sea level. Even the highest peaks in Ireland, at around 3,250ft (1,000m) above sea level, are modest by European standards. But the uplands of Ireland have a certain wilderness quality which has something to do with the richness of their wildlife and a lot to do with their emptiness. The more spectacular ranges are in the west: the Magillicuddy's Reeks and the Brandon–Slieve Mish range in County Kerry, the Twelve Bens in Connemara and the Derryveagh Mountains in County Donegal. In the east, too, there are mountain ranges above 1,625ft (500m), such as the Mourne Mountains in County Down and the Wicklow Mountains stretching away to the south of Dublin city.

Mount Brandon, near Dingle in County Kerry, was once described as 'the finest mountain in Ireland' by Robert Lloyd Praeger. In his autobiography, *The Way That I Went*, he wrote that here 'the bare rock seems so newly modelled by ice that one might imagine the glacial period had only just passed away'. The last Ice Age, to which he referred, ended some 10,000 years ago, and it was this which gave most Irish mountains their characteristic well-rounded appearance. The classic pointed summits of much younger mountains such as the Alps are rare in Ireland and are only found where a harder rock has resisted the actions of ice and weathering. Such a peak is the white quartzite cone of Errigal, visible from both the west and north coasts of County Donegal and forming its highest summit at

Red deer crossing a river. By mid-summer the stag's antlers are well grown, though still covered in a protective skin or 'velvet'. When the velvet dies and the antlers harden, the loose skin irritates the stag and he thrashes his antlers against vegetation to get rid of it.

2,466ft (752m). Among the Magillicuddy's Reeks in County Kerry, the highest peaks, such as Carrauntoohil (3,414 feet (1039 m)), are also formed of a hard resistant rock – Old Red Sandstone. This produces knife-edged ridges between one summit and the next. There are also many fine cliffs in the Irish mountains, formed through folding and faulting of the earth's crust over hundreds of millions of years and finally by the scouring action of glaciers during the last Ice Age. Mountain corrie lakes (known in Ireland as coom–*cúm)* often have a sheer back wall where moving ice plucked away the rocks. Vertical walls are also left where glaciers gouged out the beds of former river valleys, such as that at Glendalough in the Wicklow Mountains, and left the tributary streams as hanging valleys with waterfalls plunging down the cliff face. The extremes of temperature are more marked on mountain crags, without the insulating effects of snow, soil and vegetation. Winter frost and ice cause the shattering of this rock into boulders which fall to the base of the cliff and form a jumbled pile of scree.

True alpine or Arctic vegetation is largely absent from the Irish mountains because they are neither high enough nor far enough north. Even the mountains of Donegal in the far north-west of the country barely reach 2,500ft (750m) above sea level and they lie in the warm, wet airstream from the Atlantic Ocean. Lack of soil and unstable conditions on the quartzite summit of Errigal, the highest peak in Donegal, allow only dwarf willow and rigid sedge to survive from among the typical Alpine group of plants. Rainfall and wind are much more significant features of the upland climate, with the higher peaks in the west of Ireland receiving over 80 inches (2,000mm) of rain every year, about twice the average rainfall in the Central Plain. The thin soils of the mountain tops are generally waterlogged and typically support many mosses and liverworts. The summit of Lugnaquillia, the highest peak in the Wicklow Mountains, is covered in a blanket of peat which supports mosses, bilberry and other low-growing plants on an isolated cap of schist rock. Sheep-grazing on this surprisingly gentle peak has

Ben Bulben in Yeats country, County Sligo, is Ireland's table mountain. The cliffs are formed of horizontal beds of limestone which have eroded to form massive scree slopes at the base. The mountain top is flat and covered with blanket bog.

Carrauntoohill, the highest peak at over a thousand metres, is surrounded by several other summits in the Macgillicuddy's Reeks, the highest mountain range in Ireland. Glaciation has moulded the Old Red Sandstone rocks here forming many dramatic features.

Raven chicks in the nest. Breeding early in the spring to coincide with the lambing season, the raven is a very successful scavenger of carrion in the hills. A single sheep or deer carcass could mean the difference between life or death for these chicks.

produced a relatively lush carpet which is like a springy mattress underfoot.

Even the most unstable boulder scree has some encrusting growths of lichens and, where there is a flow of water, mosses and liverworts. Crevices and ledges may be wide enough to trap a small amount of soil and provide a foothold for a few stunted trees of oak, holly or rowan, out of the reach of grazing animals. In the Mourne Mountains of County Down, frauchan (bilberry or blaeberry) grows in the scree slopes on Slieve Donard, which rises some 2,796ft (850m) above the waters of Dundrum Bay. Near the summit, large slabs of stone are arranged in long stripes alternating with patches of frauchan, the plants giving a blue colour when seen from the distance. The small blue frauchan fruits ripen in August and their harvest was traditionally a time of celebration. Until about 1950, a large prehistoric cairn on the summit of Slieve Croob in the Mourne Mountains was the scene of a large gathering on the first Sunday in August. As well as the berry-picking there was much music-making, dancing and frolicking in the heather and it is said that 'many a lad met his wife on Blaeberry Sunday'.

I remember sitting one spring day amongst the fresh green foliage of bilberry, high in the Wicklow Mountains, when I was attracted by the deep croak of a raven overhead. Looking up, I could see the wedge-shaped tail in silhouette and the 'fingers' formed by the widely spread primary feathers on the bird's wings. This largest member of the crow family is such a familiar inhabitant of the Irish uplands that I always expect to see at least one pair during a walk in the hills. But this raven was behaving differently. It was being mobbed by a faster-flying peregrine which was trying to drive it out of

the territory. Again and again the peregrine dived on the raven while the larger, less mobile bird twisted and ducked in a valiant effort to out-manoeuvre the falcon. The air was pierced by the shrill calls of the peregrine until it was joined by its mate and together they succeeded in chasing off the raven. Such encounters are commonplace in late winter around the traditional nesting crags, and many peregrines breed in old raven nests which they have taken over. The ravens' constant use of the same sites year after year often gives rise to the belief that a particular raven is several hundred years old. In southern parts of Ireland, some ravens have even been given an individual name, such as *Dónal Dubh* (Black Donal), reflecting the supposed longevity of the bird. Whenever I have cast any doubt on that conviction, I have been told that 'There are people in this area whose grandfathers remember that same bird nesting every single year, without a break, on that same ledge, and isn't that very raven still there?'

Despite the competition between peregrines and ravens for the best nest sites their diets are quite different. Peregrines hunt only live bird prey, such as pigeons, while ravens specialize in scavenging for carrion such as sheep carcases. A master of the air, the peregrine is also a symbol of conservation success, having now largely recovered from the population crash of the 1960s which was caused by organochlorine pesticides in the food chain. A few pairs did survive in the more remote areas and these have helped to recolonize all of the traditional nest sites (or eyries) and many new, much more accessible locations. Quarries, both active and disused, are now widely used with apparent success by nesting peregrines. There is a disused quarry,

Peregrine falcon feeding chicks. The peregrine often takes over an old raven's nest, at times expelling its former occupants. The best nest sites are on the traditional mountain crags but as the peregrine population recovers, more accessible sites such as ledges in quarries, are frequently colonised.

beside the road near Gorey, County Wexford, which in midsummer, at the time of fledging of the young eyasses, regularly attracts crowds of passing sightseers.

I have always found the peregrine falcon a most exciting bird to watch and on many occasions I have been privileged to be within only a few feet of a ledge where the adults were looking after their chicks. Being so close to the thrilling action of such shy and wary birds of prey is worth all the weeks of preparation in carrying gear up the steep mountain slopes and setting up a hide. I have often sat crouched in one for hours while trying to obtain the best possible pictures without disturbing the main actors. As with all our birds of prey, the female (falcon) peregrine is the larger of the pair and, from my observations, she seems to be the one in charge of all the nesting activities. I have noticed that the male (tiercel) never seems to stay for long at the nest if the falcon is already there. He just drops the prey for the chicks and then leaves the ledge without delay. The tiercel is away from the eyrie most of the time, either hunting for food, which will be brought to the falcon, or standing guard on another crag some distance away. The amount of hunting carried on by the female during this time varies with individual pairs or with particular circumstances such as shortage of prey or bad weather. As the chicks develop, the falcon perches on another part of the cliff where she has a clear view. It is most interesting to watch the reaction of the young birds when they realize that food is on the way. They hear the male's call from afar as he streaks towards the cliff face and they immediately begin their own wailing chorus. As in any growing family, the shouts for food become louder and less musical as the youngsters become older.

The larger birds of prey are now mostly part of Irish history although their traditional nest sites are preserved in place-names such as Eagle's Rock above the Lakes of Killarney and Hollow of the Eagles *(An Uile Gharbh –* The Rugged Elbow*)* on the island of Inis Icíleáin, off the coast of County Kerry. From the writings of Robert Ussher and Robert Warren (*Birds of Ireland*, 1900) we know that golden eagles were widespread up to the mid-eighteenth century but declined rapidly thereafter owing to shooting, trapping and poisoning which accompanied the arrival of modern sheep management. At least fifty pairs of the white-tailed sea eagle also nested in Ireland in the last century and they must have been an awe-inspiring sight as they soared among the islands and crags. The remote coastal cliffs of Mayo in the north-west provided the last nest site of the sea eagle (in 1898), and the last golden eagle also nested in Mayo about 1912. The same onslaught of persecution in the late nineteenth century also caused the extinction of the buzzard as a bird of the Irish mountains, but it managed to regain a foothold on the north-east coast of County Antrim in the 1950s. The chalk and basalt cliffs of Fair Head and Rathlin Island provided the springboard for a slow but steady recolonization of the north and east of Ireland. By the early 1990s there were almost 150 pairs breeding, mostly in Antrim, Derry and Donegal. I have always found it strange that in the Welsh mountains, just a short distance across the Irish Sea, buzzards are so common that they hunt on roadside verges, yet they are still absent from the majority of Irish uplands. The spread of the buzzard and, indeed, the return of the eagles to Ireland, may rest largely in the hands of sheep farmers, many of whom still use poisoned baits to kill foxes and crows at lambing time. All the larger birds of prey rely heavily on carrion, especially in winter. While ample habitat and food are available to them, the chances of untimely death from poison are still far too high.

In my regular filming expeditions in the Wicklow Mountains I often find myself wading through boggy pools and tramping along peaty tracks which have a soft, springy feeling underfoot. On these paths I regularly see the distinctive footprints of badgers which remind me that, although there are no earthworms in these acid soils, there are plenty of other tasty creatures living among the peatland vegetation. Most of the Irish uplands are covered with a thin blanket of peat lying directly on the bedrock or mineral soils. The peat began to form thousands of years ago when rainfall in the mountains was even higher than it is today. The wetter parts (where the bogs are still growing) are still dominated by mosses such as *Sphagnum* but most of the Irish mountain bogs are now more grassy or heathery in character owing to the loss of cattle and the arrival of sheep.

One of my favourite times of year to walk in the mountains is August, when the heather clothes the hills in a mass of purple flowers. Large areas of the Wicklow Mountains and the Mourne Mountains in the east of Ireland are covered in dry, heathery moorland, with the delicate flowers of ling heather most numerous. On steeper, well-drained slopes the larger and brighter purple flowers of bell heather become dominant, and in wetter patches a third species, cross-leaved heath, is plentiful. Thousands of years of grazing-pressure by deer and sheep have converted many mountain slopes from heather to grassland. But, unlike in the species-rich limestone grasslands of the lowlands, only a few grasses can survive on the high slopes where the soils are poor and often waterlogged. Sheep's fescue and common bent are two mountain grasses especially favoured by grazing sheep. They tend to avoid a third species, mat grass, which is rather tough and wiry and has a whitish appearance in winter. As a result of overgrazing of the more palatable grasses, mat grass has spread at their expense and the hill-grazing has become even less productive than it was before. On wetter slopes there are mixed communities with various sedges, mosses and grasses such as tufted hair grass and purple moor grass. The latter is conspicuous in damp flushes especially on saddles between peaks and the lower valley slopes where it is well grazed by sheep and deer.

Walking from one summit to the next, I am very likely to have to cross at least one difficult patch of bog surface where erosion has removed most of the vegetation cover and the rainfall has left deep channels and gullies. The peat 'haggs' which are left standing in between the gullies are usually covered with extensive greyish mats of the moss *Rhacomitrium* and often little else. It is easy to imagine that this erosion could be caused by too much trampling, overgrazing, or some other human factor. However, recent research in both the Wicklow and Donegal Mountains has shown that eroded peat has been washing into small mountain lakes for the last 3,000 years. This rules out recent human disturbance as the underlying cause. It is more likely that climatic changes over this long period have caused the peat to become unstable and simply to flow downhill. However, there is no doubt that increased grazing pressures in the hills have been detrimental to heather moorland. On Clare Island, off the west coast of County Mayo, I

An Irish hare sheltering from the prevailing winds. With ears alert for the slightest sound of danger, the hare is ready to take off across the mountain slopes at high speed using a network of well-marked pathways through the vegetation.

have met old people who remember a time in the early years of this century when sheep grazing on the mountains was difficult because the heather was so tall that animals could not be seen. In 1903, Robert Lloyd Praeger climbed the slopes of Croagmore, the highest point of the island, and he described it as an area where heather prevailed to the summit, old and shaggy and up to a 3ft (1m) in height. Today the slopes are badly overgrazed by sheep, which have replaced cattle, and there is now extensive soil erosion. Not surprisingly, this has also meant the loss of some rarer plants, such as lesser twayblade, which were associated with the heather moorland.

Walking across a mountain slope, I am often startled by the sudden darting shape of a hare as it leaves its form or resting place with an unexpected burst of speed. My first encounter with hares was when, as a schoolboy, I went chasing them with my friends in the mountains. There was never the slightest chance that we would catch one, especially with the variety of dogs that we 'collected' on our way to the hills. When the dogs picked up the scent we would climb to the top of the mountain and watch this inexperienced bunch of cross-bred hounds yelping and howling and, at times, bumping into one another, as they went in pursuit of the hare. The fleet-footed lady of the mountains follows a very familiar path along the heather-clad slopes. A healthy hare on its own ground is a match even for a greyhound. I am glad to say that my later encounters with the hare were more peaceful and far less disturbing to the countryside. Getting close to a hare, in order to photograph it, is itself a thrilling experience.

As it bounds away, I get a fleeting glimpse of its beautiful reddish-brown

coat, one of the characteristics which makes the Irish hare a distinct subspecies of the Arctic or mountain hare. Although brown hares from Britain were introduced in north-west Ireland, they never managed to spread to the rest of the country and they may have died out by now. The Irish hare remains the only species on both lowlands and uplands, from sea level to the highest summits. It is related to the Arctic and mountain hare of Europe which turns white in winter to match its snowy surroundings, but winter whitening is only partial in Irish hares so that they remain camouflaged against the purple moor grass and heather. The pure white hare which I filmed on an island in Clew Bay, County Mayo, was an albino which remains white all year, and according to local fishermen these hares are a regular occurrence there. Its snow-white fur was in complete contrast to the other hares nearby, and I am sure it was picked off more easily by a predator.

In Irish folk tradition a malicious woman was believed to take on the form of a hare in order to steal the dairy profits of her neighbour. Another common legend tells of how a farmer grew suspicious when the milk-yield of his cows diminished greatly. He stayed up at night to watch his cows and saw a hare come to drink from them. His dog followed the hare but could only manage to draw blood from its hind-quarters as it fled. The farmer followed on and, coming to a house, asked an old woman who lived there if she had seen a hare pass by. As she answered, he noticed that the woman was bleeding and from this realized that the hare had in fact been her. Of course, real hares are entirely herbivorous and, whilst heather forms the major food source of Scottish mountain hares, their Irish cousins seem to feed on a

Red grouse in heather. The reliance of the bird on this one plant may be the reason that grouse are so scarce in Ireland. Ideally the grouse needs a patchwork of old and young heather, but large areas of moorland are being converted to mountain grassland and forestry.

wider menu of mountain vegetation including sedges and woody plants as well. It is said that Irish hares are more sociable than their British cousins, although I have rarely seen more than two or three together in the hills. By contrast, when I made a film about wildlife at Dublin Airport, there were dozens of hares grazing the open grasslands between the runways. Perhaps this has something to do with the level of fertilizer used on lowland grassland and its high productivity when compared with moorland vegetation, as well as the lack of cover.

Research at Glenamoy, County Mayo, in the north-west of Ireland, has shown that the quality and quantity of heather on western Irish blanket bogs are so low that it can support only a few grazing animals. The surface peat has been so heavily leached by the heavy rainfall (over 80 inches or 2,000mm per year) that it contains few of the minerals such as phosphorus, calcium, potassium and nitrogen which are so important for plant growth. Heather grows much more luxuriantly in eastern Ireland in the Wicklow Mountains (where the annual rainfall is about half that in the west), and this is the area in which I have seen by far the greatest number of red grouse. They usually burst from cover with an explosion of rapid wingbeats and a loud repeating alarm call, then glide away over the tops of the heather and out of sight. The Irish red grouse, which has a paler red-brown plumage than its Scottish relatives, was once considered to be a separate subspecies, found only in Ireland. However, recent taxonomic work has shown it to be a member of the Scottish race, which itself is a subspecies of the circumpolar willow grouse.

The unique relationship between the red grouse and heather moorland was recognized many centuries ago, but most of the large estates containing grouse moors in Ireland were then owned by absentee landlords and used for occasional shooting expeditions in the autumn and winter. Even as early as 1850, William Thompson noted that 'grouse numbers have been gradually decreasing from various causes connected with the operations of man'. Shooting-bag counts suggest that after 1918 numbers of grouse shot in Ireland declined significantly, and by 1945 grouse shooting as a sport had virtually disappeared. With the foundation of the new Irish Free State and the departure of the absentee landlords, there was no longer an incentive to maintain grouse stocks for shooting. For the red grouse is almost totally dependent on the heather plant throughout its life cycle. It breeds in the dense cover of older heather and feeds on the emerging shoots of young heather especially in areas that have been burned. Fire is a natural part of the ecological cycle in heather moorland, and controlled rotational strip-burning, so widely practised in the Scottish moorlands, can be used to produce a mosaic of suitable habitat types with artificial high grouse populations. Studies of captive grouse at Glenamoy showed that there was no difference in breeding performance of Irish and Scottish birds in artificial conditions but that in the wild moorland winter losses and chick mortality were directly related to the low population numbers.

One of the techniques sometimes employed to boost breeding populations of game birds in the mountains was the systematic destruction of all possible predators including fox, stoat, hooded crow, raven, magpie and all birds of prey. Professional gamekeepers were never common in

Ireland but the activities of a few, combined with the poison used by sheep farmers, was enough to cause the extinction of eagles and buzzards in Ireland in the nineteenth century. The hen harrier, a large and conspicuous raptor of mountain and moorland, was also thought to have become extinct in Ireland in the early twentieth century. But a few pairs had hung on in the Slieve Bloom mountains in the south midlands and on the borders of Counties Waterford and Tipperary. As these raptors were nesting in either deep heather or furze, any of my filming operations had to be carried out with the utmost care for fear of disturbing the birds and making them forsake the nest. The individual birds varied a great deal in their reactions to human intrusion; whereas some of the female hen harriers would disappear quietly when the nesting area was approached, others would scream and swoop at any human seen in the vicinity. The fox is a real danger to ground-nesting birds and, being a curious and opportunistic animal, is bound to follow any tracks or openings created in the heather. It was found that its inquisitiveness could be discouraged by placing obstacles such as branches of prickly furze bushes at any point of entry to the nest. I found on more than one occasion while filming hen harriers that the male bird became unavailable for pictures by simply perching on my hide, 6 inches (15cm) above my head. I suppose I should have taken it as a compliment that the bird accepted my temporary dwelling as part of the landscape!

The smallest of the Irish raptors, the merlin, is also one of the most difficult to see on its upland breeding territory. It traditionally nests in deep heather and hunts low over the ground, chasing small songbirds. I have often found the distinctive clue to the presence of a merlin in the pile of small feathers left behind on a rock or fence post after the prey has been plucked. In County Wicklow, merlin breeding sites are usually in the lower flanks of the hills where moorland and hill grazing land are intimately mixed. But in recent years much of the heather moorland here has been replaced by conifer plantations and these tiny raptors have increasingly taken to nesting in trees on the edge of the plantations. Almost invariably, they use the old nests of hooded crows, ravens or, occasionally, sparrowhawks. In the western blanket bogs of south Connemara, I have seen merlins breeding in the stunted oak and holly trees which survive on the lake islands scattered across this wild landscape.

I remember once watching a merlin hunting a meadow pipit across a stretch of bogland in Connemara. The odds were against the panic-stricken pipit as it wheeled, twisted and dodged in its efforts to escape from its streamlined aggressor. At every turn the merlin kept getting closer to its prey and I could see that the battle was almost over when the pipit suddenly swerved and flew into the only available piece of cover, a large clump of furze. The merlin, which was intent on catching its prey, didn't, or couldn't, stop as it chased after the pipit. What happened next was totally unexpected, and so against the odds as to be almost unbelievable. The meadow pipit escaped out of the far side of the bush while the unfortunate merlin flew straight into the jaws of a waiting fox! I can only presume that the fox was sleeping in the furze bush when he was rudely awakened by all the commotion and quickly pounced on the merlin before it could extricate itself from the prickly branches.

There are probably more meadow pipits than any other bird per square mile of Irish mountains. Wherever I walk in summer, they fly up from the heather, but in winter they move to the lowlands where food is more plentiful. They usually nest in a tussock of grass and sing their high-pitched song from the air. This is much shorter and less attractive than the song of the skylark and when it is finished the pipit parachutes down to its nest on stiff wings. By comparison, breeding waders are quite scarce on Irish mountains although there are a few pairs of golden plover and dunlin in summer on the wetter upland ranges of Donegal and Mayo. Both species are

at the southern limit of their European breeding range in Ireland and are much more numerous on the tundra habitats near the Arctic Circle. More widespread in Ireland is the curlew, although in recent years it has declined in mountainous areas, with the loss of open moorland, and is now mainly restricted to lowland bogs and damp pasture.

I am always impressed by the sight of a herd of red deer grazing quietly on a mountainside as these are our largest native land mammals. I take great care in stalking deer in the open hills as they are sensitive to the slightest noise or movement which is not familiar to them. It is of course vital to

Burning heather, Sugarloaf Mountain, County Wicklow. Farmers use fire as a tool to burn off the heather and encourage the more productive grasses favoured by sheep. Heather can regrow following a fire, but finds it hard to compete with the more vigorous grasses and the intensive grazing which follows.

A merlin plucks its prey, a meadow pipit. This the smallest of the falcons, nests in heather or forestry plantations and hunts small birds on the lower ground where prey populations are higher. Like the peregrine it is vulnerable to the effects of persistent chemicals in the food chain.

move upwind towards them as otherwise they will catch my scent and move rapidly across the hillside, their light brown rump markings showing clearly, until they feel a safe distance from me. Then they will turn to watch and listen until this human intruder passes through their home range. My favourite time of year to watch the deer is October, when the rutting season is in full swing. Like a company of theatre players, the mature stags take up their territories and bellow defiantly at one another. Each stag rounds up a harem of females (hinds) and spends much energy in defending them against rival males. During this time he will wallow in wet areas of ground and roll in his own urine which gives him a characteristic smell. Real fights between the stags are not common and most of the disputes are settled by posturing, roaring and thrashing of vegetation with the antlers, which leaves the challenger in no doubt about which is the stronger animal. After mating the stags and hinds separate and remain as discrete groups until the following year. The hinds remain on the higher ground until bad weather or food shortage drives them to seek the lower ground or shelter of woodlands. The majority of calves are born in May and June and for the first few days the newborn animal is left alone to lie well camouflaged in cover, the mother returning only briefly to feed it. Within a week or two the hinds with calves have rejoined the main herd, which is usually led by an older, experienced female in late summer. The stags especially suffer a good deal of irritation from flies which buzz around the velvety antlers and to avoid them they often move to higher, windy ground in hot weather.

Red deer remains appear in some of the earliest known human

settlements in Ireland, such as that at Boora Bog in County Offaly which is dated at about 8,400 years ago. These early settlers would have used all parts of the animals with bones and antlers fashioned into tools and other useful items like combs. The skins were used for clothing and hides for temporary dwellings while the meat was probably boiled in cooking pits known as *fulachta fia,* the remains of which are widespread in Ireland. The destruction of the native woodlands up to the seventeenth century, and the increase in human population in the eighteenth and early nineteenth centuries, drove the remaining red deer into a few isolated places in the more mountainous areas of Ireland. Here they survived only on one large private estate which is now part of the Killarney National Park. In the mountains of Donegal red deer were reintroduced to the estate of Glenveagh in 1897, the stock being supplied from collections in County Down and County Wicklow as well as from Britain. That year the fence around the property was completed making it the only enclosed deer forest in Ireland where the deer were kept for private shooting parties. The fence was breached in the 1920s and many deer escaped to the surrounding hills, but Scottish specialists were brought in by a new owner in the 1930s to repair the fence. The estate is now part of the Glenveagh National Park and holds one of the largest herds of red deer in the country. In County Wicklow red deer have interbred extensively with the introduced Japanese sika deer and all are now hybrids of mixed genetic stock. As a result, some herds of deer that I see in the Wicklow Mountains may include animals of all sizes and almost any shade from the russet coat of the red deer to the dark brown shades of sika.

Although they are a natural part of the ecosystem, deer populations can have significant impacts on habitat, especially in the absence of natural controls such as large predators. At high densities they can cause heather moorland to be replaced by mountain grassland, but in Ireland such gradual changes can be blamed more on selective sheep-grazing. More obvious effects of the deer are seen in some of the upland woods where winter

Meadow pipits are by far the most common birds in the uplands of Ireland. They nest on the ground and use gorse (or furze) bushes as vantage points from which to spot insect food on the ground. They themselves become prey for several of the raptors as well as foxes and stoats.

grazing slows regeneration of oak, birch and holly. In forestry plantations deer will browse some species of young conifers and strip bark from older trees, reducing the economic gains from commercial forestry.

The mountains provide some of the few remaining areas of open, unfenced landscape in Ireland. When I visit the hills I always experience a sense of freedom in the wide, unrestricted views, of delight in the clear fresh air and of refreshment in the clean, bubbling water of a mountain stream. Increasing numbers of urban dwellers are learning the pleasures of a day in the mountains and, with growing amounts of leisure time, a few mountain areas near the cities are now used by large numbers of visitors in summer and on fine weekends. As a result of this disturbance some sensitive mountain birds such as curlew have disappeared entirely from a few of their former breeding haunts. In the most disturbed areas deer often move on to higher ground at weekends, returning to the better grazing on lower slopes when the visitors have gone home. Improved roads, some developed originally for forestry, allow the penetration of visitors' cars into areas which were previously remote from traffic noise and fumes. Long-distance walks have been developed in many counties but in some areas these cross sensitive vegetation and the presence of too many people in such areas can cause serious erosion. With the thin soils and high rainfall on western mountain slopes, unrestricted growth in sheep numbers can easily upset the delicate ecological balance and cause further erosion. Extensive areas of heather moorland are disappearing under blankets of sitka spruce as increasingly attractive financial inducements are offered to farmers to switch from rough grazing to forestry. Similar conflicts of mountain land use have been resolved in other countries by good planning and control of damaging developments. In Ireland the National Park concept is used only in its narrowest sense where land owned by the State is managed for conservation and amenity purposes. Nevertheless, some of our most spectacular upland areas such as those around Killarney, County Kerry, Glenveagh in Donegal and parts of the Wicklow Mountains are now protected in this way. The future for the mountains lies in multi-purpose use but sensitively planned and managed by people who understand the importance of these remote and beautiful habitats.

The clear waters of a mountain stream are a priceless asset in an increasingly overpopulated and polluted world. Upland streams have the cleanest freshwater although many are quite acid due to the underlying rocks and peaty soils through which they flow.

8

THE UNOFFICIAL COUNTRYSIDE

*I return to the mud at Grattan Bridge, feeling I am rapidly
approaching that stage of dejection which drives the strong-minded to a
public-house, when from low down in the western sky there comes a gleam
of yellow light, rapidly broadening and brightening. And then suddenly
five great swans appear, flying down the centre of the river.
In perfect formation, long necks outstretched, broad wings beating in
unison, they sweep by majestically, a vision of beauty, gleaming plumage
all snowy against the old houses opposite. While I still watch their receding
forms fading into the smoky mist, a low red sun bursts out from
underneath the last bank of cloud. It floods down the river; the long vista
of dull houses lights up in a dozen lovely shades through a faint pink
haze; the spires and towers behind stand up transfigured; the dirty water
turns to gold and silver. One gazes at a dream city, beautiful
beyond belief. And while I stand, a breath of softer air, bringing
with it hope and a lifting of the spirit, comes from the west;
the wind has changed.*

Robert Lloyd Praeger,
A Populous Solitude, 1941

*Waders roosting at sunset in a busy
industrial area. Despite the noise,
disturbance and pollution associated with
urban areas, many wildlife species live
in cities and towns, adding to the quality of
life for their human residents.*

Dublin Bay in winter with migratory wildfowl in the foreground and snow-covered hills in the background. The location of the city between the mountains and the estuary provides a wonderful range of habitats for wild plants and animals.

There seems to be a natural inclination on the part of town folk to be associated with nature in one way or another. Many city people take a great interest in wildlife and avail themselves of every opportunity to enjoy it wherever it is found. In recent years wildlife organizations have taken advantage of this situation by encouraging the public to take a more active part in preserving important habitats in their own area. City schoolchildren who have little opportunity to visit the country have been made aware of the wildlife found in parts of their city such as waste ground and they have been taught how to use the school yard as a nature-study area.

Although I have never lived in a city, my days of working in the centre of Dublin many years ago were my first introduction to its plants and animals. Being a wildlife enthusiast is like having membership in a club, where members keep in touch and news of worthwhile observations are reported regularly by other devotees. I remember the magpie often being mentioned in city dispatches. Sometimes it was a pair building in a tree opposite a convenient upper-floor window, where they could be photographed, and I was invited to use the house as a hide whenever I liked! But more often it was a plea for help. Many city people were upset by the magpies' raids on small birds' nests although this predation is quite natural in the wild. Other wild animals were more welcome in city gardens and were actively encouraged to stay. I knew one lady who always had a family of hedgehogs in her well-sheltered garden and they were given daily feeds as payment for keeping the slugs at bay. Some of the city's wild residents became so well known that they soon became celebrities. Every year a mallard duck nested

in the grounds of the *Dáil* at Government Buildings, a site which had the minimum of disturbance and the maximum of security. The staff were well aware of their responsibilities to this bit of parliamentary wildlife, and there was the guarantee of an official escort for mother duck when she and her very young family of fluffy ducklings would waddle from the nest site out through the main gates and across the busy street on their way to the nearby pond in St Stephen's Green. It was an extraordinary sight and people were always impressed when a tall policeman on duty at the entry to government headquarters, would walk out on to the street and hold up Dublin's traffic for this seasonal avian procession.

At first sight, cities and towns may appear to hold few opportunities for wildlife among the concrete and tarmac, the noise and fumes. But many plants and animals have adapted to these conditions and some thrive in close proximity to people. These may include some survivors from the original countryside such as the orchids growing on a railway embankment. There are also the opportunistic species like urban foxes and magpies, colonizers which have moved in to take advantage of the new habitats created among our dwellings. Inevitably, there are many sensitive wild habitats and species which cannot survive the disturbance caused by urban development. But a surprising range of wildlife exists in Irish cities and towns, and an understanding of its needs can make a valuable contribution to the quality of urban life.

As the medieval city of Dublin began to grow from its original nucleus in the Viking encampment on the south bank of the River Liffey it was totally

Fitzgerald Park, Cork. Despite the formal layout of urban parks, their leafy habitats provide a refuge in the city for many woodland birds. Trees and hedges form valuable nest sites while the extensive areas of grass and bare soil are used by many birds for feeding.

Top: Kingfisher. These attractive river birds can be seen from the footpath which leads along the banks of the River Lagan, through the centre of Belfast. Using familiar perches they drop vertically into the water to catch small fish such as sticklebacks and minnows.

dependent on the surrounding countryside including the wooded hills to the south. Game such as red deer and wild boar from these woodlands provided an important source of food for Dublin's earliest inhabitants, although the hunters had to compete with wolves and other now-extinct predators such as eagles. Fish, shellfish and wildfowl from the nearby estuaries were also part of the staple diet in medieval Dublin and their importance is immortalized in the traditional song about Molly Malone who sold 'cockles and mussels, alive-alive-o'. By the seventeenth century the growth of the city was accelerating and intertidal areas of Dublin Bay were being reclaimed to house and feed the growing masses. Around the walls of the city were a number of 'greens' or areas of common grazing. One of these, St Stephen's Green, survives today as the most popular public park in the city. Sir Ralph Payne Gallwey, author of *The Fowler in Ireland* (1882), was told how a young law student in the early nineteenth century could take his gun and walk over the marsh in what is now St Stephen's Green to 'add a dainty snipe to his dinner'.

During the second half of the twentieth century there has been a drift of population away from the rural areas of Ireland towards the growing conurbations of the east coast. In the 1960s most of the satellite villages in County Dublin were separated by large areas of farmland and the distinctive sound of the corncrake was common in summer even in suburban areas up to the 1970s. But the city of Dublin has expanded to cope with the rush of people to the 'big smoke'. Like an ageing heather plant, it has decayed in the centre but continues to spread outwards. About one million people (nearly one-third of the population of the Republic of Ireland) now live in the Greater Dublin area, whilst the population of Northern Ireland is heavily centred on the Belfast area.

Belfast, in the opinion of Robert Lloyd Praeger, who grew up there, 'stands pre-eminent in Ireland for the beauty and variety of its environment' *(The Way That I Went)*. The shipyard gantries, which played such a prominent part in the growth of this northern city, are today still silhouetted against the backdrop of Cave Hill, just a few miles away. From the south-west the River Lagan flows through a well-wooded valley to the red-bricked city streets and beyond to the shores of Belfast Lough. A footpath follows the riverbank from Stranmillis to Lisburn, several miles upstream, allowing the public to see kingfishers and otters in the Lagan Valley Regional Park. In west Belfast, between the Falls Road and the M1 motorway, an area of marshy grassland known as the Bog Meadows holds breeding lapwing, snipe and mallard, with corncrakes reported from here as recently as the mid-1980s. Despite all the changes which this great city has seen, some of the original countryside upon which it was built still survives inside its boundaries.

So, too, in the towns of Galway, Limerick, Cork and Waterford, each built around the estuary of an important river, there are fragments of the natural habitats which once sustained the first settlers on these sites. In each case, the old city centre also contains a variety of transient habitats – on derelict sites, disused railways and canals, and in the dockyards. In Dublin's inner city there are a huge number of vacant spaces, with an estimated 56 hectares in a 'derelict state' in 1981. Around this time, members of the

Bottom: Small tortoiseshell butterflies feeding on a buddleia, or butterfly bush. This vigorous introduced plant is one of the primary colonisers of waste ground and derelict buildings in the city. It grows on walls and window ledges and even sprouts from disused chimney pots.

Top: Starlings roosting on an electricity pylon. Thousands of chattering birds crowd together at night for warmth and safety in numbers. They may also use these night-time roosts to share information on good sources of food.

Middle: Pipistrelle bats. Summer roosts are often in the attics of buildings but, as winter approaches, they move into underground tunnels and cellars where the temperatures are stable and they are safe from disturbance. Vapours from the chemicals used to treat roofing timbers can be lethal to the bats.

Bottom: A male herring gull stands guard as his mate incubates the eggs in a nest on a thatched roof. Such man-made substitutes for cliff-top sites have only recently been exploited as the year-round supply of food from refuse dumps and fishing ports has allowed the population to grow.

Dublin Naturalists' Field Club took on the task of documenting the plantlife of the city centre, and their results were published as *The Flora of Inner Dublin* (1984). In the eighty years which had elapsed since Nathaniel Colgan's *Flora of County Dublin* (1904), much of the former 'green belt' of Dublin had been consumed by concrete and tarmac. But, to the surprise of Field Club members, many habitats and plants of great interest survived. There were limestone grassland flowers growing on railway embankments, wetland species in the canals and even small areas of woodland habitat in some old undisturbed gardens.

Old and crumbling walls in Dublin city are an important habitat for ferns, especially where broken drainpipes keep them constantly wet. Praeger found that 'till some unfortunate tidying up had been done at Leinster House (the seat of the Irish Parliament), male fern, broad buckler fern, soft shield fern and hart's-tongue flourished in the angle between it and the National Museum' (*The Way That I Went*). Today, the commonest plant on old city walls is the *buddleia* which also sprouts from disused window ledges and chimney pots – anywhere that can hold a small pocket of soil or crumbling mortar. In summer, its large mauve flowers attract swarms of bees and hoverflies as well as some of the larger migrant butterflies such as peacock and red admiral, which have given it the alternative name of butterfly bush. *Buddleia* was introduced from China as a garden plant but it seems to have found a niche in our city walls with its ability to spread masses of seed and to grow rapidly ahead of the competition.

One winter evening, I was waiting at the Central Station in Belfast for a bus to take me home. In the gathering dusk, the sky overhead began to fill with flocks of starlings, each small party arriving from a different direction. One by one the flocks coalesced until a huge mass of birds circled in the sky like a whirlwind, with thousands of individuals flying in formation. Suddenly, as if in response to a signal from a flight commander, the entire flock dived down into the darkened warehouses of the dockland area where they arranged themselves in chattering rows along the steel girders beneath the roofs of these massive buildings. Summer roosts are usually smaller and often situated in trees. I once had a telephone call from a tormented manager of one of Dublin's leading hotels who had thousands of starlings roosting in the trees which ringed the hotel car park. His prestige guests were horrified when they emerged from the hotel functions to find their status symbol cars covered in bird droppings. Everything except tree-felling had been tried and failed to dislodge the starlings. The problem eventually resolved itself, for the autumn leaf-fall removed the starlings' cover and they moved to roost in buildings elsewhere in the city. Older classical buildings with plenty of ledges are preferred, the steeples of city churches being favourite sites. The noise of thousands of starlings jostling for positions inside an old church can be quite deafening.

Bats also roost in old buildings but their comings and goings are much less obvious than those of the starlings. They work the night-shift and emerge, usually one by one, as dusk descends. These warm-blooded mammals feed entirely on flying insects, catching them on the wing by a technique of echo-location similar to the radar systems used by aircraft. As a tiny bat swoops overhead along a shady street or hedgerow, the rapid clicking sound is only just audible above the background noise of traffic. The human occupants of buildings are seldom aware of the presence of a day-time bat roost in the attic unless it becomes so large that the twittering voices can be heard in the house below. In a traditional bat roost there may be a pile of droppings several centimetres thick on the attic floor but this rarely causes a problem as it is naturally composted over time. There are just seven species of bat in Ireland, although several of these are more abundant here than anywhere else in Europe. The pipistrelle is the commonest and also the smallest species. The largest is Leisler's bat, which is common and widespread in Ireland. This species, together with the lesser horseshoe bat, which is confined to the west and south-west of the country, are internationally endangered and are considered to be our most important mammals. One of the threats facing the bats is the re-roofing and repair of old houses, which can mean the closing of the gaps they use as entrances. The persistent chemicals used to treat roof timbers against woodworm and fungi are known to emit poisonous vapours which can kill roosting bats.

For some birds, city buildings are a perfectly suitable substitute for natural cliffs and caves. Feral pigeons nest on the window ledges of office blocks in the same way that their coastal cousins, the rock doves, use sea cliffs. Similarly, the roofs of coastal buildings provide herring gulls with all the necessary security for nesting that they would get high up on an offshore island. In the fishing port of Howth, County Dublin, these large seabirds nest every year among the chimney pots of housing estates near the harbour and their noisy and aggressive behaviour has not endeared them to the local residents. Similar behaviour has been observed in Waterford and Galway, where the artificial supply of food from fishing port and refuse dumps has allowed the gull population to grow beyond the capacity of the naturally available nest sites and spill over on to the roofs. However, their habit of feeding on human refuse also has its drawbacks, with frequent outbreaks of a fatal disease called botulism causing some large colonies of herring gull to decline in recent years. This has been linked to the build-up of bacteria in stagnant water and decaying rubbish, especially in the black plastic sacks, which are now used for virtually all domestic waste.

Most attempts to dislodge nesting gulls from their adopted homes have failed, but occasionally city buildings are used by much more sensitive birds. In 1987 a pair of peregrine falcons was regularly seen together hunting feral pigeons in Dublin's dockland. In 1988 they began to roost together hundreds of feet above the streets on a disused gasworks, one of the highest buildings in the centre of Dublin city. The falcons were using the steel platforms and walkways to pluck their prey which included pigeons, starlings and waders caught on the shores of Dublin Bay. The gasworks, which was formerly used to store manufactured gas, had become disused since natural gas replaced town gas in Dublin, and maintenance visits to the site had been reduced to a minimum. However, there was nowhere on the structure which was completely secure from disturbance, so the Irish Wildbird Conservancy together with the Dublin Gas Company erected a small wooden nesting platform on the side of the gasworks. Peregrines had previously nested on shipyard gantries and industrial buildings in Belfast and, based on experience with captive-bred falcons in North America, the platform was filled with gravel and peat to simulate cliff-top soil. There was no development in the following years and it seemed that the falcons regarded this man-made ledge as quite inferior to the natural equivalent. Then, in 1992, beneath a dramatic photograph on the front page of *The Irish Times*, it was announced that there were two large chicks on the nest platform, and Dublin had joined an elite club of cities with peregrine falcons breeding in the city centre.

Dublin's dockland was already well known in ornithological circles because it had been used since at least the 1950s by nesting common terns. These graceful seabirds, which normally breed on offshore islands, found that stockpiles of coal used to fuel the Poolbeg Power Station provided just the right conditions of bare ground while the security fences prevented access by ground predators such as foxes. The terns became quite aggressive in defence of their nests and dived on any human intruders, even striking passing dock workers on the head. Once again, the conversion from coal to natural gas was the catalyst for change and the terns were forced to find other spaces. They subsequently nested on reclaimed land awaiting development and in a fenced-off car park where only thistles grew among the gravel.

The Dublin Naturalists' Field Club noticed that there is a successional cycle in the wild plants of waste ground from its clearance until it is developed. In the first year after disturbance the main colonizers of the bare ground are annual weeds such as shepherd's purse, chickweed and wall barley. In the second year vigorous exotic plants such as sycamore, *buddleia* and Japanese knotweed take root, and in following years clovers and perennial grasses arrive to form a closed community similar to rough pasture. Few areas of derelict land are allowed to develop to a climax vegetation, but occasionally scrub comprised of sycamore and willow gets a foothold. Near the Poolbeg Power Station in Dublin's docks an old tiphead of industrial flyash became disused in the 1980s and was turned over to Dublin Corporation for development as an urban wildlife area. Now, in summer, walkers from nearby Sandymount are accompanied by the seemingly endless singing of skylarks. A pair of kestrels, which nest in a disused building nearby, regularly hunt over the rough grassland areas, hovering in the sky with widely fanned tails as they search the ground for small mammal prey. The docklands of Belfast Harbour are dominated by shipyard gantries and extensive refuse dumps which have gradually filled in virtually all the upper foreshore around the city. The reclaimed land of the harbour estate includes a number of brackish water lagoons which have become quite important as high-tide roosts for waders such as curlew and oystercatcher and as breeding places for a variety of ducks.

Trees have many important functions in the urban environment. As well as their visual and architectural values they provide us with shelter from wind, rain and noise. By filtering dust from the atmosphere and by producing oxygen they improve the quality of air for people as well as for wildlife. Trees can also prevent erosion of topsoil by binding it together with their roots, by intercepting rainfall with their leaves and by increasing the ability of the soil to absorb moisture with the addition of leaf litter. As habitats for wildlife in towns trees have a vital role to play because they

provide food and shelter for mammals, birds and insects, nesting places and songposts for birds, and an opportunity for some of the original wildlife of the ancient woodlands to live on in urban areas. Many of the trees planted in towns and cities are introduced species such as horse chestnut, sycamore and flowering cherry, and while these are not as rich in wildlife as native species such as oak, ash, willow and hazel, they provide many of the structural benefits of natural woodland. Blackbirds, for example, thrive on the woodland edge. When Ireland was covered with dense forests blackbirds were probably confined to the edges and to scrubby clearings around lakes and rivers. They nest in dense shrubbery and use tall trees as territorial songposts but they prefer to feed in open areas of grass on soil animals such as earthworms as well as on autumn fruits and ivy berries. Mature suburban gardens and parks provide all these requirements and have probably helped blackbirds to spread over a much wider area than would have been possible in the original forests.

For many birds urban trees also provide safe night-time roosting places, out of reach of traffic or prowling cats. Dublin is famous for the large roost of pied wagtails which gathers on winter nights in the trees along its widest thoroughfare, O'Connell Street. Like the queues of Dubliners waiting for the cinemas nearby, the birds trickle in from all parts of the city until a thousand or more of them are twittering in serried ranks along the bare branches. The same sixteen plane trees have been occupied by these birds every year since at least the 1920s, when James Joyce was writing his famous works of fiction on life in Dublin. Then, as today, they come here to seek refuge from the cold because the city-centre microclimate is a degree or two warmer than in the surrounding countryside. The wagtails, which are known to suffer higher mortality in severe weather, exploit the large amount of waste heat from city buildings and vehicles in order to survive. Their numbers reach a peak in the colder months of December, January and February, and in severe winters the birds crowd into the more sheltered trees in the middle of the street. At Christmastime the trees are decorated with bright lights illuminating the wagtails for all to see and providing some extra central heating for the birds.

The trunks and branches of older trees are often covered by a patchwork of lichens which prosper in the absence of competition from ground vegetation. Lichens are not just single organisms but consist of a partnership with fungal threads supporting unicellular algae. Because lichens have evolved very efficient means of absorbing chemicals dissolved in the air they act as excellent indicators of air pollution around industrial and urban centres. In the most heavily polluted city centres trees are often devoid of all lichens because the sulphur dioxide in the air disturbs their sensitive metabolic processes and they die. Lichens are divided into three main groups, shrubby, leafy and encrusting species, the latter being the most tolerant of polluted air. An early study around Belfast found that as well as the variety of lichens increasing in cleaner air, the area of tree trunk covered by lichens increased from almost nothing in the city centre to over 70 per cent at 10 miles (16km) away from the worst pollution. More recently, the distribution of lichens has been used to map the air quality around urban and industrial areas. Sometimes, as in Cork, hilly land in the city alters the

Outside the General Post Office in Dublin city centre, pied wagtails roost in the same line of plane trees every winter. They benefit from the slightly warmer temperatures in the city and disperse in the morning to feed on roads and riversides.

typical concentric pattern of lichen distribution. Sheltered valleys can also provide a 'protected' area for the more sensitive lichens close to an urban area. One such 'lichen oasis', with very sensitive species such as *Ramalina*, was discovered in an alder swamp close to the southern boundary of Cork city. On the east coast, there is a 'lichen desert' around Arklow owing to the poor air quality caused by a large fertilizer factory, and parts of Dublin city are devoid of all lichens.

The level of smoke pollution in Dublin became critical during the 1980s, with national or European Community standards breached on average about eleven times each winter. The main cause was the traditional burning of solid fuels such as coal and peat on domestic open fires. In very cold weather a temperature inversion occurred and the smog was trapped over the city for days on end, causing serious respiratory illness in the human inhabitants, damage to historic buildings and probably serious disruption to sensitive plants and animals. A ban on the sale and distribution of smoky

coals was introduced in 1990 and, together with increasing conversion of domestic heating systems to natural gas, a marked improvement has occurred in Dublin air.

Many of the small birds which breed in Ireland migrate in autumn to warmer southern latitudes but, for those which remain, winter can be a testing time. Shortage of food is the main cause of death and this becomes critical in late winter if there is a prolonged period of snow and ice. When people in towns and cities put out food in their gardens for the birds they are helping to sustain the more vulnerable populations until the spring. The species which take advantage of these free handouts, mainly tits, finches, thrushes and starlings, are much the same as those in the rest of northern Europe, but in Ireland there are no woodpeckers or nuthatches. Members of the crow family are regular garden visitors, rooks, jackdaws and magpies being among the most numerous.

The magpie is a relatively recent arrival in Ireland: there are many literary

Brent geese feed on a golf course in Dublin Bay. As the city expands to cover their intertidal habitats these arctic breeders have adapted well to urban life. They exploit a number of amenity areas including football pitches and public parks but the quality of feeding here is inferior to that on the shoreline.

Badger cubs being fed in city suburbs. The city has grown to envelope former areas of countryside, forcing their former occupants to scavenge in the streets and gardens. Badgers live underground in traditional 'setts' and their nightly forays follow familiar routes to known food sources.

references to its absence up to the seventeenth century. There is even a written account of the arrival of a small flock of magpies in Wexford, in an easterly gale about 1676. From here they are believed to have spread to the rest of the country, so successfully that by the reign of George II (1727–60) a statute was enacted offering a reward for their destruction. In this century magpie populations have increased markedly with the decline in persecution, and the spread into urban areas has undoubtedly been aided by the modern concern with landscaping and tree-planting around new developments. The nests are substantial structures with a dome of twigs over the top to prevent robbery by aerial scavengers. Their loud, chattering call is a warning to others of the same species and there is much chasing and fighting during the breeding season. Nesting density of magpies in parts of Dublin is almost four times that recorded on farmland, which suggests that they are exploiting a good food supply in town. While there is much emotional blame attached to magpies for raiding the nests of smaller birds, studies suggest that these form only a small part of their diet and that soil animals and plant material are their main food items. Perhaps the huge increase in domestic refuse, in easily opened plastic sacks, has provided another all-year source of food.

Animals are quick to learn where a regular supply of food is to be found, and this has worked to their advantage in many cities and towns. Armchair naturalists have taken account of this situation and tempt a variety of mammals and birds to come to where they can be viewed in comfort from the living-room window. Badger and fox-watching evenings are now a

regular pastime in parts of Dublin. This can cause some problems if the next-door neighbour is not a wildlife enthusiast and is more interested in tidy flower-beds and a well-manicured lawn than burrowing mammals. I filmed a whole family of badgers which had been visiting a garden in Bangor, County Down, for several years. The elderly couple who had adopted the badgers kept the activities of the animals a secret in order to ensure their safety. The local shopkeeper who lived just around the corner must have wondered at times how the couple's household pets, a budgie and a miniature poodle, could possibly be eating so much stale bread every day!

The Dublin Naturalists' Field Club found that the grounds of large institutions in the city often provide a refuge for woodland species which may have survived since the days when the countryside reached right up to the city walls. In the more shady parts of St Brendan's Hospital typical woodland plants such as tutsan, herb robert and greater stitchwort are found. Many of our public parks, like St Stephen's Green in the centre of Dublin, were laid out in the last century when there was a passion among wealthy landowners for collecting exotic trees and shrubs from all parts of the globe to assemble in collections or arboreta. Such parks often included artificial ponds which were stocked with exotic waterfowl. 'Feeding the ducks' in St Stephen's Green is such a regular habit of Dubliners that the density of mallard and moorhens here is much higher than on any natural lake. Those which manage to nest successfully in this busy park often have their young ducklings snatched from the water by hungry gulls which are also attracted by the abundance of bread. In Cork city a small freshwater

Mute swans on the pier at Kinsale, County Cork. Large numbers of non-breeding swans gather to exploit food sources such as sewage outfalls and waste from factories. They can survive in quite polluted waters but oil damages the waterproofing of their plumage.

lake called the Lough has been surrounded by suburban housing and is now used as public park. Owing to the high level of artificial feeding a large flock of up to 200 mute swans visits and feeds in the Lough. They spend about one-third of their time feeding on bread supplied by local people. Nearer the coast, sportsfields in St Anne's Park in north Dublin are regularly grazed by brent geese when the tide covers their estuarine feeding grounds on the mudflats around Bull Island. The geese have become so accustomed to walkers and their dogs that they are not disturbed by them but simply move around the fields until the tide recedes.

Dublin's Phoenix Park, at 1,750 acres (708 hectares) one of the largest enclosed urban parks in Europe, has been a walled deer park since the seventeenth century. The fallow deer which range among the woodlands and open grassland are descended from a herd introduced in 1662 and have coexisted for centuries with major events such as horse racing, cycling and religious gatherings. For most of the year the broad-antlered bucks and does with fawns roam in separate herds, coming together for the rutting season in October. The Park's woodlands provide good breeding sites for sparrowhawks and long-eared owls, both of which hunt the abundant songbirds in suburban gardens outside the Park walls. Urban foxes also find the park a good base for mounting raids on suburban dustbins. They seek out the remains of fish and chips discarded on the pavements by late-night revellers and finish off the petfood dinners left by overfed cats. There is such an abundance of waste food in the city that urban foxes rarely die of starvation but they do suffer a higher mortality owing to road accidents. The President's House, *Áras an Uachtaráin*, is set in a well-wooded estate within Phoenix Park. Foxes are regularly seen here crossing the lawns near the house. This was probably the base from which they raided the ornamental ducks in the neighbouring Zoological Gardens. I remember one fox in particular making daily raids on the zoo's wildfowl collection. Matters became so serious that the superintendent instructed his keepers to capture the elusive robber, before any more ducks or geese disappeared. An early-morning watch was organized and the fox was located as it made its way towards the pond, looking forward, no doubt, to another good zoo breakfast. The keepers almost succeeded in surrounding the fox, but it made off and hid above the polar bear enclosure. As the hunting party approached, the fox left its hiding place and looked for an escape route. Keepers were now blocking its way on all sides, as it ran along the top of the wall above the bears' pen. The only open area was on the side directly above the enclosure, where the bears were watching the activities with more than a passing interest. Nobody expected the fox to go in this direction, and whether it slipped and fell or jumped in panic we will never know, but one of the polar bears was as quick as lightning and caught it almost before it had landed on the ground. That was the end of this particular zoo raider!

The centre of Dublin city is usually defined by the ring created between Phoenix Park and the two canals, the Royal and the Grand. These waterways were built in the late eighteenth century to link Dublin's docks with the River Shannon in the midlands. The Grand Canal has remained open to barges, but the Royal Canal fell into disuse in the early years of this century and was closed to navigation in 1961. The long period of neglect

has allowed a variety of wetland plants to become established on the canal banks, with reed canary grass and sweet reed-grass forming great thickets of cover for nesting moorhen and mallard. Tall plants such as meadowsweet, yellow iris and wild angelica brighten up the banks in summer with their large, showy flowers. Close to the water's edge are mare's-tail, water mint and fool's watercress as well as the poisonous water dropwort. Canadian pondweed and the yellow water lily float in the water where a century ago they would have been swept aside by the passing barges. On the banks of the Grand Canal there are planted osier (willow) beds which were probably originally used for thatching and basket-making. Today the canals provide quiet, tree-lined pathways on the old towpaths and a corridor for aquatic wildlife to reach into the city from the surrounding countryside.

The breeding places of mute swans on Dublin's canals are so traditional that local people can remember nests in the same locations since at least the 1930s. It is popularly believed that there were no swans on the River Liffey before 1924 when a pair was released at Islandbridge by the writer Oliver St John Gogarty. This much-publicized event was known as his 'offering of swans' in thanks for a rescue from near-drowning at the same location, and it is said that all the swans in Dublin today are descended from this one pair. In reality, swans were frequent on the Liffey in the eighteenth century but may have become very scarce in the nineteenth century when shooting the birds and raiding their nests was common practice. Now they nest widely on canals, riverbanks, ponds and even estuarine salt marsh, although the breeding success in such places as the Broadmeadow estuary is much lower

Urban foxes are now a familiar sight in many Irish towns and cities. They survive on the contents of dustbins and discarded dinners outside take-away restaurants. City life also has its hazards as many foxes are killed or injured by road traffic.

than on freshwater. Urban swans seem to suffer many more accidents than their country cousins. Collisions with overhead cables are commonplace, especially where these cross waterways. The swans sometimes land mistakenly on wet roads and are found wandering among the traffic, unable to take off again. In October 1986, a large flock of more than fifty swans was feeding quietly on the River Tolka in north Dublin, when an oil spill occurred upstream. The entire herd was oiled and had to be taken into care and treated to prevent poisoning. The swans' plight caught the sympathy of the public and there were many donations of food and money to help maintain the birds. One by one the majority were rehabilitated and released and the herd began to reassemble on the same stretch of the River Tolka where the oil spill occurred.

Thankfully, things have changed and these worst days of city pollution are coming to an end. But the importance of urban areas for wildlife is likely to increase as the countryside comes under even greater pressure from development. The growth of more sympathetic attitudes to nature conservation can only be fostered if people have a chance to experience wildlife in natural surroundings close to where they live. A century ago most Irish people lived in rural homes but today over half the population lives in towns. There is a growing concern for more healthy living conditions, to improve the quality of the air and water on which we depend. As well as ensuring improvements to the human environment, the town planners of the future will need to leave space for the plants and animals which inhabited the landscape before people arrived and which will probably survive long after we have gone.

Mallard duck nesting in a car park. Despite the pressures of life in town, there are many quiet corners which are used by wildlife species. Nature is quick to recolonise any disused land and the oldest developments have the greatest diversity of habitats for wildlife.

Further reading

Bellamy, David, *Bellamy's Ireland: The Wild Boglands,*
Country House, Dublin, 1986

Brown, Robert, *Strangford Lough: The Wildlife of an Irish Sea Lough,*
Institute of Irish Studies, Queen's University, Belfast, 1990

Cabot, D. (ed), *The State of the Environment,*
An Foras Forbartha, Dublin, 1985

Curtis, T.G.F. and McGough, H.N., *The Irish Red Data Book: 1 Vascular
Plants,* Stationery Office, Dublin, 1989

D'Arcy, Gordon and Hayward, John, *The Natural History of the Burren,*
Immel Publishing, London, 1992

de Buitléar, Éamon (ed), *Wild Ireland,*
Amach Faoin Aer, Dublin, 1984

de Buitléar, Éamon (ed), *Irish Rivers,*
Country House, Dublin, 1985

Evans, E. Estyn, *Mourne Country,*
Dundalgan, Dundalk, 1978

Fairley, James, *Irish Whales and Whaling,*
Blackstaff Press, Belfast, 1981

Fairley, James, *An Irish Beast Book,*
Blackstaff Press, Belfast, 1984

Feehan, John, *The Landscape of Slieve Bloom,*
Blackwater, Dublin, 1979

Heery, Stephen, *The Shannon Floodlands,*
Tir Eolas, Galway, 1993

Holland, C. H. (ed), *A Geology of Ireland,*
Scottish Academic Press, Edinburgh, 1981

Hutchinson, C.D., *Birds In Ireland,*
T. and A. D. Poyser, Calton, 1989

Jeffrey, D.W. (ed), *North Bull Island: A Modern Coastal Natural History,*
Royal Dublin Society, Dublin,1977

Lavelle, Des, *Skellig: Island Outpost of Europe,*
O'Brien Press, Dublin, 1976

Further reading

MacConghail, Muiris, *The Blaskets: A Kerry Island Library,*
Country House, Dublin, 1987

McCracken, Eileen, *The Irish Woods Since Tudor Times,*
David and Charles, Newton Abbot, 1971

Mills, Stephen, *Nature in its Place: The Habitats of Ireland,*
The Bodley Head, London, 1987

Mitchell, Frank, *The Shell Guide to Reading the Irish Landscape,*
Country House, Dublin, 1986

Mitchell, Frank (ed), *The Book Of The Irish Countryside,*
Blackstaff, Belfast, 1987

Ó hÓgain, Daithí,
Myth, Legend and Romance: An Encyclopedia Of The Irish Folk Tradition,
Ryan Publishing, London, 1990

Praeger, R.L., *A Populous Solitude,*
Hodges Figgis, Dublin, 1941

Praeger, R.L., *The Way That I Went,*
Hodges Figgis, Dublin, 1937

Robinson, Tim, *Stones of Aran: Pilgrimage,*
Lilliput/Wolfhound, Dublin, 1986

Roche, Richard and Merne, Oscar, *Saltees: Islands of Birds and Legends,*
O'Brien Press, Dublin, 1977

Tubridy, Mary and Jeffrey, D.W., *The Heritage of Clonmacnoise,*
Trinity College Dublin and Country Offaly VEC, Tullammore, 1987

Ussher, R.J. and Warren, R., *The Birds Of Ireland,*
Gurney and Jackson, London, 1900

Whelan, Ken, *The Angler in Ireland: Game, Coarse and Sea,*
Country House, Dublin, 1989

Wyse Jackson, Peter, and Sheehy Skeffington, Micheline,
Flora of Inner Dublin,
Royal Dublin Society, Dublin, 1984

Index

Picture Acknowledgements

Liam Blake
Frontispiece

Cian de Buitléar
71, *166*

Éamon de Buitléar
8-9, 13, 14, 15, 19 top, 22-23, 24-25, 35, 36, 38-39, 44, 50-51, 56-57,
63, 64, 65, 67, 68, 69, 70, 78-79, 80-81, 82, 87, 90-91, 92, 95, 96, 99 both,
100, 101, 102-103, 107, 115, 126-27, 129, 130-31, 132, 138, 140-41, 142,
143, 148, 158, 162-63, 164, 170, 173 bottom, 180-81, 185, 186

Frank Doyle
133, 154, 155, 159

Richard T Mills
7, 10, 20 middle, 26, 31, 32, 40-41, 42, 43, 45, 47, 48 all, 53, 54, 55,
58-59, 66, 72, 74, 75, 84, 88, 93, 108, 111, 113, 114, 116-117, 119, 120 all,
122, 135, 136, 139, 144, 147, 150-51, 152-3, 165, 169, 171, 173 top,
174 all, 178, 182, 183

Richard Nairn
16 bottom, 60, 125, 137

Bernard E. Picton
16 top, 18, 19 bottom, 20 top & bottom, 28

Nico Rippen
118